# Facing It

**Elizabeth Walter**

Copyright © 2023

# Dedication

To my husband Timothy and our two children: Savannah and Isaac, who walked by my side throughout this story, intimately witnessing my 20-year demise, as they stood by helplessly, but not without hope. As the tears stream down my face, I am reminded of all I put you through and what was returned back to me. I was a grave burden, filling your lives with grief, yet, in return, I was given all of your support, your devotion, your forgiveness and your unconditional love. I am humbled by your daily mercies and constant encouragement. My mind lacks the words necessary to properly thank you. I love you…too much.

To those who have a hold of my heart, although they have left this world: my brother, Mike, my grandma Alvina and my nephews, Landon and Jeremiah. I know you are expecting me, as I have been washed in the precious blood of Jesus, just as you are. I miss you all and wish you could have known the new me.

To my extended family, who have been there for me, overflowing with compassion and grace. Thank you for loving me through.

To Terry and Terry White: Thank you for caring for Jordan throughout his wonderful life with you. You gave him everything he could ever need. Mind, body and soul. You fed him daily with your unconditional love. You have been amazing parents and for that I am eternally grateful.

To Jordan: Thank you for being you. I was blessed with carrying you as God knit your heart and body together within my womb. Giving you away was painful; knowing that you would be brought up in such a fine home brought me little peace in the beginning. Through the years, I could see the great life you had through the pictures your parents would send me and I became content knowing that you were loved. I hope that you know that everything I did was out of my pure, innocent love for you.

To the people of Rustic Hills Church: Thank you for never giving up on me even when I had given up on myself.

To the handful of people in my life who have known my story and yet withheld judgment. Although this group of family and friends were keenly aware of my circumstances, our relationships did not falter. They accepted me with outstretched arms and an open mind, while doing everything within their power to help me. Because of these people that were willing to sacrifice themselves for my sake, I have come to learn that love can heal brokenness. Love navigated me through years of feeling lost. It comforted me when the cold, dark blanket of depression smothered me with its heavy embrace. Love pushed me to go on another day when I felt worthless and was without hope. Love healed me.

To all that I have dedicated this book: Thank you for loving me through my story. I am grateful that you taught me what love is so that I can say with confidence, I truly love you back.

Love never gives up, never loses faith, is always hopeful and endures through every circumstance...Three things will last forever-faith, hope and love-and the greatest of these is love.

I Corinthians 13:7&13(NLT)

# Acknowledgment

To my Lord and Saviour, Jesus Christ, who was here with me during those dark, early morning writing sessions. He put the fire in my soul to tell my story with purpose, giving me His strength when mine was depleted. He has given me a new identity. I am loved by God. On those days that pass by and thoughts of worthlessness fill my head, I remember who loves me. He is enough. Following his lead, I was able to begin this journey of recording my life exactly as it played out. He has fitted me with great hope that it will help others, as he has bestowed upon me the courage to release my story for the world to see. I would never have thought this book was a possibility. But through Him, all things are possible. He broke my heavy chains and now I am walking free.

"You don't have a soul. You are a soul. You have a body."

C.S. Lewis

# Contents

# Foreword

Follow me, so he left what he was doing, and followed Jesus.

What if Jesus were to approach you right now, at this very moment in time, wherever you are reading these first few words? He is beside you, and as He lays His grace-filled hand on your shoulder, you gently turn your head. You recognize Him. Then He speaks to you. "My yoke is easy and my burden is light," With His spoken words, you know that this is your Shepherd standing before you now. With His outstretched arm, He softly says to you, "Follow me." At the pure awe of His holiness, you are brought to your knees. He joins you on the ground, placing his loving arms around you as you weep in humbleness and humility.

Every single person has their own story. Every life is viewed from a distinct perspective. He has determined our times before they are appointed. He knows the boundaries of each of our dwelling places. When I began this writing endeavor, I thought all the words of my life could be contained in a small book. One of those seventy-page short-reads. I could never have known the path that the Lord was leading me down. This entire process. Waking up early morning, spending precious fellowship with the One who saved my soul.

Rather than an autobiography, it is more like a diary. Holding within its pages all the secrets never told and all the emotions that lay hidden deep within my soul. I soon began to sense God moving in my life as our time together increased. Being present with one another deepens our relationship with each new day together. Towards the end of this book, these chapters of my life, I realized I was writing about my past while I was still living out the pages that would be contained within this very binding. Not only was my writing therapeutic. Now, it had become another fork in my road, as Jesus, once again, whispered gently in my ear, "Follow me." With tears falling off my cheeks, I took his hand, and we began to walk together. Hand in hand. Papa with His princess. That's how I feel in His Presence. He has held my hand, with great strength at times, down the path of the beautiful struggle that brought me to where I am today. I am redeemed.

In the following pages, I am giving you a window's view into my life experiences, along with my most disturbing thoughts and my most intense feelings. The value of the written word is like an intangible treasure. As my fingers stroke the keys of my computer, I am bearing my very naked, vulnerable soul to you. I felt God leading me to write my story of His redeeming grace. A tale that needs to be told. So, to whoever is reading this, "I hope we can walk through my journey together. I'll sit by you if anything is sad or scary. I promise."

"Follow Me.", Jesus told him. So he got up and followed Him.

Matthew 9:9

# Chapter 1

# Hope

Does your heart long for a book that is real and naked, and raw? These pages contain the true story of my twenty-year journey, traveling through the darkest of forests, dragging my family behind me, sharing in the extreme suffering as collateral damage. Guilt and shame consumed me as we trudged futility through the thick underbrush. This book contains fiercely graphic pages. It is not for the light of heart. I know that it was through my ever-present Lord that I am able to write this book today. He has saved my life that I am present for today and my everlasting life with Him for tomorrow. I have left the mud, the muck and the mire simply by placing my hand in that of my Savior's and falling, exhausted, into His open arms. He wraps them around me in His love. He is fully aware of every breath that fills my lungs. He knows that I can be a sinner. And I can be a saint.

I am not writing this book as an authority on theology or on the basis that I have been redeemed, making my life perfect. I am so very far from perfect. But I am so perfectly broken. A wretch has been saved. I remain in desperate need of My Savior's mercies daily. This autobiography doubles as a story of redemption through Christ. My chains have been broken, and I am living out the freedom Christ gave me. Now joy and love are my constant companions, even though the storms and struggles life brings. This is the beautiful story of how He changed me. It was painful to write much of its contents. But I believe it is a chronicle of history that needs to be told. So Jesus asked the man, "Do you want to be made well?" A question my Lord asks me daily, through this, my beautiful struggle.

# Chapter 2

# One West Harmon Drive

I hate this chapter. It is void of information that tells the beginning of my story. Writing it has brought me much distress, as I hate revisiting this era. But it did exist and has become a part of who I am. I do not give you, the reader, a true explanation of those years encompassing my childhood. This is more of an introduction of some of the main players in my young life.

I begin my story surrounding the span of time of those precious, innocent years when every little girl believes she is the center of a (mostly) sunny world. Although throughout those formative years of mine, I had seen my share of thunderstorms. I have been flooded by the rains as they've come pouring down. Realistically, let me just say I lived a childhood where I never asked anyone to check for monsters because I knew they were there.

As a young girl, I found myself enjoying country life and sucking the very marrow out of nature's precious bones. We resided in an altogether perfect homestead a few miles from town, bordering Lake Mitchell, in a surprisingly nice house. The only thing my mom got in the divorce settlement, I'm told. As a child, I fondly remember swimming in the cool lake or building sandcastles in the warm sun during summer vacation. In the cold winter months, I would entertain myself by sledding down our slick, bumpy snow hill and ice skating once the lake had frozen to a great thickness. During any day of the year, I could be found foraging through the thicket of trees in a wide ditch by our house. I would treasure my time alone as I would quietly wander through the seemingly gigantic forest of trees, listening to the birds chirping in the sky overhead. Scents from the fresh herbs and seasonings that mother nature was cultivating would fill my senses as I strolled through the familiar territory. It was a peaceful place to let the shadows free, and growing up, it became my sanctuary.

My hometown is your typical backward-thinking, gossip-riddled small town. Those kinds of towns where people pause with their grocery carts parallel to each other, "Just talking" … nowadays I suppose it would be equal to texting a coworker or using Facebook to message a friend…all about the atrocities occurring at 1 West Harmon drive…my home address. My childhood resembles an ongoing tumultuous storm. One in which the gravel flies in your face with great force from the high winds that almost take you off your feet as the skies darken from dark gray to black.

It is likely that someone observing this storm would be very eager to seek safety inside their own home, perhaps even deep within the walls of their basement, to ensure the safety of their family and themselves. Stay on that soft pseudo-cushion, neglecting the obvious need and their instinctive role as a decent member of society to fulfill it. "Well, now, what could I do?" They would think inside their self-righteous, small-town brains.

These horrific Hippocrates! They seem all too aware of my family life when I first meet them, although they are strangers to me.

I can see them looking at me with those thought-filled eyes. "Poor child." I could hear them whispering a notch too loudly, one to another, all about the reality I was living in…yet no one came out to our house to comfort us. No guidance was given. No services were offered. No complaints were filed in our defense. No feathers were ruffled. No well-meaning intention of any of those people on any given day transformed into any real provision or actual support of any kind. That would have required submission of self for the benefit of another. The brand of sustenance that would obligate the giver to get their hands real dirty. People don't tend to gravitate toward messy situations. I passionately realize at this early age how little people care for anything "unclean." I was likewise aware that in this small town, even as this sweet, pint-sized, cute, little tomboy, I am not particularly cared for.

People would greet us with whispers and stare at me in such a way that it stirred some feeling within me to look down. Kept my head down a lot those days…to avert their pompous, derogatory glares that I knew were drilling a hole into the back of my head as we passed by. Instead of taking preventative measures, those naive people were too busy eagerly gossiping about the next disaster my family would face, ignoring the inevitable blowback that such a disaster would cause.

"Bastards!" I would think. A word that I learned as I heard it spoken out of my grandma's mouth when she was super pissed.

As a child of the 70s, you learn to keep secrets and not create a ruckus over injustice or cause a fuss when you've been hurt or violated. "Sticks and stones may break my bones, but words will never hurt me." That was the extent of my elementary school's entire anti-bullying campaign. They were different times...the twilight zone different.

I was the last born in my family, with four siblings and our mom all living under the same roof. The person missing from this equation is this narcissistic ass who had our bite-sized town sheriff and deputies in his back pocket. The entire police squad was scared of him. He is psychotic, with a level of evilness so deep within him that it often made me wonder if the gape of souls was empty as he breathed in his. The men in blue would brush off the entire episode. I didn't see him as my dad, nor did he see me as his child. I never knew why he couldn't just stop coming out to tame his anger. For real, though, most of the time, my grandma would use that "b" word in reference to him. Because of the absence of a father, my oldest brother, Michael, was forced to step in as the man of the house, and he played father figure for me during those first several years of life (and forever after). He was the sole reason we had our one big family vacation to the Gulf of Mexico, staying with his friend's family. A young man named Fausto Nolasco whom Mike had met at Outward Bound. A cold weather survival camp that they both shared a passion for. His friend invited my brother to bring his family down anytime. That next summer, Mike took him up on his offer and made the trip's itinerary without hesitation. My entire family possessed so many emotions encompassing that journey we labeled as our summer vacation. Galveston, Texas. Very hot and even more humid.

The van's engine began cutting out while driving south on the interstate. My reliable, protective brother decides to pull off the road to investigate. Approximately two hours North of the Texas border, in a modest cowboy town, I watched as my brothers simultaneously struggled to find the cause of our engine problems. Mike thought it might be the van's alternator. I surveyed them, working together intensely in the unforgiving Southern summer heat, as the sweat dripped off their faces like rain. After a while of observing the makeshift mechanics, I drifted off to the tall, thick weeds in the ditch of the road, thinking how it felt like I was inside an oven.

As I walked along, I prayed to God to have mercy on us. I came before the Lord, as an innocent child, asking Him for His miraculous help. Two hours later and with a Good Samaritan's play-by-play instructions, my brothers had that rusty, old van's engine humming! It had never sounded so capable. It roared to life as Mike gave it gas.

I Gave a "Hallelujah" in that densely foliated ditch. I praised my Lord for bringing us the good samaritan who took his time to stand by and direct my brothers as they laboriously replaced our alternator. Also, we only reimbursed the man for the part, and that was on Mike's perpetual insistence. Throughout their conversation, he told us that he had driven by us on his way to run an errand. If we were still there when he was on his way back home, he had promised himself he would stop and help. And he was a man of his word. It's stunning to think of how such a small amount of that good samaritan's time, an afternoon…would make such an impact on my entire vastness of days that I am now writing to you about him 45 years later. I see him as a man used by God through the power of my prayer and the willingness of this precious stranger's servant's heart.…for when we broke down, he helped us change our alternator. {Matthew 25:35-40}

We were all exhilarated as we jumped into our van. Only three more hours, the final leg of our uncomfortable traveling conditions. I took my seat on top of the puke green engine cover that contained the newly restored engine that was purring beneath me as we drove. My brother went a little over the speed limit to arrive there just as quickly as we could. He had a cargo of people that were ecstatic to meet these new friends of his.

Moreover, we were eager to take a nice deep breath of that fresh ocean air. To unpack our things and get a drink of anything wet. But greatest of all, we all wanted to get out of this bona fide oven on wheels. We arrived at his new friend's house without a hitch. We all fought to be first out of the hot van. Leaping out the door, it felt so good to stretch my legs, knowing we were at our vacation destination.

Fausto Nolasco and his family were amazing hosts. His little sister and I became fast friends, as we were the same age. We are like two peas in a pod. Having noodles of fun and oodles of giggling. I remember whispering endlessly to each other until we would fall asleep each night. The mom and dad made quite an impression on this young girl within me. Her mom was an amazing cook. Fresh hot tamales. I had never experienced so many of my taste buds being served at the same time. Her dad impressed me simply by being the dad. We all enjoyed our vacation to the beach. I got lost while searching for pretty seashells to place in my small red bucket with fragile hands. My brothers body-surfed and my sisters tanned and looked at boys. We all had lunch together. We sat in the shade, under the canopy the dad had set up and ate the food the mom had prepared for our picnic basket. Food tastes extra delicious when you are a five year old girl who is worn out from swimming, searching for sea shells and playing in the sand. It was an all-around awesome vacation. And it is in my permanent memory file marked as

"Happy."

Without my brother, that excursion never would have taken place, erasing the highest peak of our happy family memory bank.

My oldest sister Michelle is a calm soul. At least she appears to be on the outside. She is ten years older than me and would sacrifice her time to be present with me, while meeting me at my level. Either she was pretending at the mock store we had created together, playing several hands of Go Fish with me, or trudging through the never-ending, unrelenting game of Candyland. Her touch is so gentle. She made me feel at peace. At the time, I was unaware of what it was. I just knew it felt nice. Around this period of history, I was just a child, so naturally, I instinctively love my entire family, but I actually like her. It's my present belief that being liked by a child says a lot about a person's soul.

My brother Sean is one of the middle children and served the purpose of a textbook scapegoat for our dysfunctional family. He was always in some sort of trouble with the law, which is pretty damn ironic when you think about it. He struggled in school. Liked smoking weed, but that was pretty much the norm back then. Weed wasn't as potent, and you could buy a dime bag from a bowling alley or any car with dark-tinted windows. At least, that's what my early purchasing experiences riding along with my brother taught me. His passion was taking anything apart. Afterwards, he would patiently put it back into one piece again. He liked to tinker.

He was my playmate growing up in the brambles. Living in the wide open country, Sean and I often constructed our special homemade kites. We would use old, black garbage bags we found lying on the sides of our country dirt road. I would gather straight, long sticks and proudly display them to my big brother. One day, as my brother skillfully brought our magnificent kite high off the ground, I grabbed hold of the extra-long tail as it dusted across my shoulder. At each moment, the enormous kite was rising higher towards the bright summer sky. To my surprise and delight, I was being lifted off the ground a bit. I held firmly onto the kite's tail as my miniature feet were skiing across the flat grassland plain, I could hear my brother proudly laughing at our awesome creation, and I saw how his eyes grew bigger as our well-constructed kite rose towards the sun. Eventually, the tail's length had expired, and I felt the last portion of it slide through my fingers, making me stop dead in my tracks. Although it lasted for just a moment, and I was off the ground just enough to barely see air under my shoes, I was most certainly flying. This will forever be one of my favorite memories of Sean and me, antiqued in time. Although I was nine years his junior, he was my favorite person to play with. My Best Pal.

Monica was the baby of the house for eight years before I came along, stealing her spotlight. She always had to have things her way, which usually meant quickly and sparkling clean. Three words that do not describe me at all, fueling our ongoing arch rivalry. But I knew that she loved me. She would bring me along on her babysitting gigs and I would go on dates with her and her boyfriend. Often, she would let me come to work with her at the art museum. I think a seed was planted there. My love of the arts flourishes to this day.

My grandma loved me, and I could feel her love in how she cared for me. She and I were like peanut butter and jelly. Whenever she took care of me, she would have something fun for me to do or maybe an adventure to go on. At times, I would help her clean her rental properties. I had my big five-gallon bucket full of whatever fresh-smelling cleaning concoction my grandma had filled it with. I would look proudly at my handiwork as she would tell me what a good "scrubber" I was.

She made me feel competent. When we got home, she always had my favorite meal ready via her slow-cooking method on the stove. "Shicken and tree small potatoes with some carrots," I could hear my grandma telling her lady friends my favorite meal for the umpteenth time with her heavy German accent. She was always so proud of me for exactly no reason at all. And I knew she was. That 70s saying is so backwards. It should be, "Sticks and stones may break my bones, although words can bring me great pain or sustain me.

I have left out the majority of my upbringing with good

cause. Some things are not meant to be recorded. I simply gave you a glimpse of my early years. The ghosts of that embryonic stage of my life still visit me nightly.

# Chapter 3
# The Vagabond

Living at our lake house those last couple of years held an ocean full of heartache for such a delicate organ that lay beating inside my chest. My siblings were leaving the house, one by one, to start their own lives. Michelle ended up moving away to some big city east. My sister Monica got married and had a little girl. Sean followed suit but had a bouncing baby boy. Mike left to be his own man as he lived his first year away from the house in the college dorms. I know he relished his newfound freedom with no responsibilities to care for except his own.

After waking up day after day, just Mom and I, with the emptiness screaming throughout the halls of our quiet, abandoned, big house, my mom finally, painstakingly decided to sell it. She and I had outgrown its memories and its hollowness. I guess a person could say it was sold before it even went onto the market. Our rich neighbor snagged it before our realtor had finished putting their sign in our yard. Full price. Jackasses. Snobby family who knew they were better than us, ensuring that they might never dare speak to us, and only looked at us as if they were looking down from their high-rise pedestal.

As kids, you deal with things differently. Living in the same house for the first ten years of my life, I was indeed aware of the sheer contempt our neighbors felt for us. My siblings and I often left a present for them by their front door. A dead, stinky fish, or sometimes a bag of flaming dog poop. Nothing dangerous, as we would watch to ensure they received our package. Then we would all quietly giggle as we walked away, crouched over to avoid being seen. We were young. We wanted to even the playing field a bit; let off a little steam. I never did like them. They made me feel like we were unworthy of living next to them. Now they owned our home, too, and we honestly had nowhere to go.

Throughout my next phase of life, my mom moved around a bit. She never seemed to be able to make enough money to support us substantially. We had lived in so many places. She had one interview that took us back to our home state of South Dakota. It was in the Black Hills, a good six-hour drive from my hometown. I remember waiting outside in the car for my mom during her interview, praying to God that she would get this job. I had known how badly she wanted it. A position in which she would be making use of her college degree, which translates into making way more money. I wanted it so terribly for her that I could almost taste it. As that last thought lingered in my mind, my mom got inside her driver's side door, interrupting my thinking process. She was talking a little louder than usual and a lot faster. She was not only offered the position she applied for but one position above that. She is being promoted, and she hasn't even started yet! What? We are moving to

Custer, y'all.

(Yahweh Yireh…the Lord who provides)

We moved virtually instantly as all we owned was packed inside the hatchback of the Plymouth Horizon my mom, and I were driving. We moved into a house on the grounds of the healthcare facility because it was unbelievably cheap rent. The place wasn't great, but I'd lived in much worse. I was happy to simply be somewhere on this gigantic map of ours.

Custer is a town bordering on two thousand people, give or take, making it the smallest place I had ever had the pleasure of living in. Being a citizen of this small town means that the entire population knows what is happening in my life before I do. In this tiny cowboy's paradise, there were limited employment opportunities. For the most part, people either put food on the table as a logging family or earn their living at the same large healthcare facility that my mom would be employed with. There was one stop light that always blinked yellow or red. The Piggly wiggly was our sole grocery store. There were three churches in the face of ten bars and saloons sprinkling the three blocks of pavement that completes the extent of our downtown. I already had my qualms about this hick, Old West town snuggled deep within the Black Hills.

Starting a new school has a plethora of drawbacks, and Custer was not my first rodeo, so I already knew what to expect. The endless chatter that I would overhear in the hallways revolving around me, the forever "new kid." Each new rumor about me indirectly enters my ears. The awkwardness I would feel as each teacher would increase my already elevated level of discomfort, calling me up to the front of the class for a superimposed, super long introduction as I stood there squirming. It never got easier being the new kid. I felt completely overwhelmed as my eyes met 30 new pairs of eyes, each set belonging to a brand new peer of mine. Each one stared back at me. Making my mind scream, "Stop!" as my mouth remained silent.

She would often prompt the students to give me welcoming applause. "Super great. Thanks." As I found my seat, I hoped the red-hot fire of embarrassment on my insides was not showing through, making my cheeks blush. Adults always seem to know how to make a bad situation worse. Maybe the children should teach while we adults sit at the school desks, procuring their ancient wisdom. (Luke 18:16) What a concept. It always took me a while to survey a new school. Eventually, I found they all had three social classifications: my friends, my acquaintances, and my enemies. Not Custer. They had two classes of people: your preps and your hoods. Now the preps came to school in their white, starched polo shirts and tan colored dockers, driving the nice, safe car that mom and dad had provided them with.

They occupied the upper parking lot. They were all in sports, almost every single one being a stereotypical jock. Some of those boys did not possess a sliver of respect for girls, thinking they owned every girl in that high school simply because of how important their inflated egos made them believe they were. Not a lot of great qualities in that set of boys. But for the most part, being a prep meant your parents had money; you grew up in a semi-normal childhood, had a passion for sports, and cared about your appearance. Essentially, about a block away, in the lower parking lot, are the hoods. These are a much tougher crowd. Long hair, some sporting a cap, others hair is a mess. One guy is bare-chested, pulling a wrinkled t-shirt out of his car's rusted trunk as he gets ready for the last bell to ring. Hoods always go in on the final bell. Their vehicles are old, noisy, and beaten up. Every other vehicle in this lower parking lot is a half to a full-ton pick-up truck, and a hunting rifle is mounted in the back window of each truck.

Being a hood also meant you were poor, so you didn't mind breaking the law to feed your family. Poaching became an essential habit for some families' nourishment. Hoods were involved in one sport: fighting! If you wanted rights to park in that lower parking lot, you had to be one tough mother.

Anticipating the start of yet another new school makes my stomach full of butterflies turn into bats swarming through my chest as my fear and anxiety rise to reach their plateau that fateful day…

# FACING IT

Outside the school doors, all the other students and I were waiting for a teacher to come and unlock the two sets of double doors so that we could all file in. Performing like good little soldiers on their first day back at training. During those painful minutes of waiting, I found my gaze meeting the ground a lot. I would look up to attempt to analyze this strange group of characters, but my advanced instincts fail me. I knew this would be a formidable school to figure out. I released a measure of my built-up tension as the teachers came, holding both sets of doors wide open, as all of us dismayed students marched dumbfounded into their eighth grade of middle school.

Complete fear overtook my primitive teenage body as I slinked into the desk of my first class. There were no new introductions unless you include the details she gave about herself as she wrote her name in cursive on the chalkboard. The chalk screeched each time she pressed too hard along the curves she drew. Her larger-than-normal frame slides down each row of desks, handing out the class syllabus. As she slaps the packet on my desk, I feel her instant distaste for me as she tries successfully not to recognize that I am a new student, even though I stick out like a sore thumb in this small, hick town.

During the break between classes, I met my locker neighbor. Jennifer Fors. The fire of my anxiety tames itself to a small roar as this new person is being nice to me. She ends the conversation with,

"We'll talk after school." But I know not to count on people's empty words. I went through my first day haphazardly. Meeting a few nice people, as well as a few assholes. Glares have met my gaze, as well as smiles. I hated most of my teachers, but I've always had this deep seeded problem with authority figures. After school, I happily head to my locker and am consciously, slowly packing up for the day and getting ready to leave. I wait until nearly every person is absent from the virtually empty hallways, and still no Jennifer. Sadly, I pushed my way out the heavy double door for a long trek to the public library.

I felt a tug on my hoodie. "Hey, I told you we'd talk after school. Do you want to come over?" Her words did mean something. I graciously accepted her delightfully surprising offer. At that moment in time, I was overjoyed. "My first day could not be going better for me," I thought. We walked to her middle-class house, complete with her sweet, cookie-cutter mom, who drove a Volvo. She and I enjoyed each other's embellished stories, giggled at our goofiness and ate to our heart's content. At that moment, she made me feel accepted. We ended up going to an epic high school football game that night. I had never been to any sporting event, unless you count watching bowlers play a round in a dark bowling alley that reeked of beer-soaked carpets and had the constant aroma of stale smoke.

But now, everything was all so new and refreshing. It was

exhilarating to watch the touchdowns, pass interceptions, and tackles while we sat in the bleachers, shivering in the coolness of sundown. We would yell, screaming at each victory, and booing if the other team had one. I would carefully mimic whatever I observed Jennifer doing. But it was okay. That was the norm for me, and I truly was having fun. Jennifer and I both remained cold as the evening temperature dropped into the night.

I offered to get us hot chocolates to help us warm up. She spotted me going down the cement stairs gleefully on my way to the concession stand. A fiery redhead, about the same stature as me, yelling obscenities at me that even I refuse to repeat with written words. Let's just say it was bad. I, hailing my hard-earned "take no shit" attitude, spurred her on by daring her to repeat herself. Now, I have advanced my movements so as to be face -to-face with her. A useful tool for intimidation. When she promptly did repeat each and every atrocity, spitting right in my face as she spoke…Pow.

Right hook to her jaw, using my back leg to ensure a more powerful punch. The fast-growing crowd encircling us is now chanting, "Fight! Fight!" louder in succession. She stumbled sideways, and with this angry look in her eyes, she swung as I kept ducking and swooping to avoid being punched back. I think she was kind of drunk, and she couldn't land one. To save face, she walked off, yelling, "Bitch", as she turned her head back towards me, so the crowd of people that had surrounded us would know who she was referring to and make it known that she had the last word. "Good initiation." I thought to myself, as I feel I have just been introduced to Custer and, in turn, Custer has, most assuredly, been introduced to me.

"Good first day." I sarcastically thought as I readied myself for the second day of my eighth-grade year and whatever blowback last night would have to wait for me. Shortly after arriving, I discovered that the fiery redhead from last night's encounter was basically the queen bee of the hoods. Walking up those bottom parking lot stairs to the front door of my school that second morning and every morning thereafter, extremely graphic language would be yelled in my direction by her and all her badass friends. Only the girls. Boys are too smart to be caught up in such caddy behavior. But those girls were certainly creative with their outbursts toward me. They were too stubborn to stop causing me trouble and I was too stubborn to go into school through a different door.

She never challenged me to another fight, though. Ever. Surprised me. Surprised the entire school body. That year, each morning, as I made my way up those stairs, my ears were bombarded with a barrage of profane insults. And I took it. Because that is who I am. A person who doesn't back down and will stand her ground at virtually all costs. I knew those girls were all bark and no bite. They proved that to me every morning. As I climbed those stairs, many words were spoken, yet never a punch was thrown. Besides that happy annoyance, the rest of my eighth-grade days were filled with teachers I disliked, subjects that bored me and new friends that surrounded me.

That summer, I worked as a waitress at a "fancy as it gets for the Hills" kind of restaurant. My eyes grew big as I saw the wad of tip money I had grasped together in my hand from the night's earnings, albeit I made $2.01 per hour. My summer went by in a blur. I worked forty hours a week and partied even more. That summer has a lot of exciting, fun memories within its borders.

The beautiful, lively summer was coming to an end, and I would soon be starting my freshman year. If you haven't figured it out already, the middle school and high school are combined in one building, so moving from middle school to high school was no transition at all. It brought me great peace, knowing that the fiery redhead had graduated and would no longer be harassing me.

Here it is, the first day back at school. The test. I'm walking towards the bottom parking lot, along the sidewalk. I get a few whistles from the boys, making my face redden. As I make my way up the stairs, I hear the wonderful sound of silence. Not absolute silence. This was the first day of a high school year. But there was no one yelling at me, nobody cussing me out or calling me fresh names. A few senior girls even said hi as I walked by them on the stairs. The test was taken and I aced it! The wicked witch has graduated! This was no longer her turf. It was mine.

Looking back, I would have to say that ninth grade was my favorite year of high school. Boys were beginning to take a particular interest in me. I made some good friends and even had a best friend. My first one since third grade. Strangely, I felt accepted by both the hoods and the preps. I genuinely preferred the hoods. These were my people. We had seen hard times, an unspoken truth among us. We knew hunger and we tasted pain, as its sweet blood drips into our lives much too often. We felt disgust as people preemptively labeled us as vagabonds. We are survivors.

My freshman year went well, although I still despise the whole concept of school. At least my social life had brightened up considerably. My sophomore year would have enough burdens within it to make up for my uneventful past year.

As a blossoming young woman, it didn't take me long to figure out that Custer also had two lovely activities available for teenage girls. Getting super drunk in the state park and letting the guy who bought you the beer take advantage of your numb half-conscious body. Lovely.

I was one of the few girls who had a steady boyfriend at the time. Imagine what a shock it was when I found out I was pregnant! I was one of the good girls that was monogamous to each of the intimate partners I have had up to this point in my short life. I was disillusioned with the belief that pregnancy only happened to promiscuous girls. As a young person, no matter the shadows of my past, I always expected the best for my life. Polly Annie's style of looking at my future. So even though it was possible, I never thought I'd become pregnant. I was two weeks late, though. "Probably just stress," I reported to my immature brain.

A tidal wave hit me with such force it brought me down to my knees, backpedaling unsuccessfully to prevent the impossibilities of my future. But there it was. Bill held onto the positive pregnancy test as I could sense the pure shock coursing through his veins. I do not recall another word being spoken between us until it was close to sunset. This was my cue to begin the mile-long walk to my house, so I could be waiting there when my mom returned from work. I felt an overwhelming need to share my news with her. Bill and I said our goodbyes, and I walked down the path to my house on a mission to tell my mother.

I wanted to leave, but she would not allow me out the door. So, I went to my bed, pulled the covers over my head and curled up in the fetal position. "That did not go over even close to as badly as I thought. Oh, on the contrary. It was much, much worse." I thought as I drifted off to dreamland. I went to bed with swollen eyes from sobbing all day. As I lay in bed that night, I prayed to God that He would just take me. I knew I didn't have the strength to deal with this.

I awoke the next morning and made my way to school. I wore what I wore the night before for pajamas, which consisted of unmatching blue sweats and a pink hoodie. I could have cared less what I looked like; it felt like my life was over. Angie, my best friend, meets me at the lower parking lot staircase with a plethora of questions. As she turns her head and finally notices me, she says in her matter -of-fact tone, "You look like shit." Thank you, Angie. That is just what I needed to hear. However, honesty was high on my character list requirements for being my best friend and her "call a spade a spade attitude is one of her best qualities.

My year-long boyfriend is there waiting with her. "We need to talk," he demands. Angie, bluntly ignoring his request, takes my hand to drag me to the first class that we are already late for. I turn my head back and yell, "Later!" to him as he stands motionless at the other end of the hallway. "He looks how I feel," I thought to myself. Angie hated my boyfriend, Bill. Reflecting, she couldn't have been more right about him! Our intense talk at lunch had no conversation. Instead, Bill righteously preached to me, "It was his baby too, and he should have half the right to say what to do with it!" At the same time, I was throwing my glass of cold, ice water in his face because I could not believe what he was suggesting.

He wanted to abort this baby! I took one long look at him in utter disgust, then stormed out of our makeshift lunchroom. That was the last time I saw Bill before we went on Christmas break, and

I certainly am not minding the silence. Gives my mind time to slow down and be more aware as my thoughts scroll through my head. My mom and I were heading back to Mitchell for a holiday, a much-needed respite for baby and me.

While staying at my sister's for our time in Mitchell, my morning sickness kicked in with a burst. "Lovely." Besides that imposition, the visit was peaceful, and being around people who genuinely love me is always comforting. It gave me new perspectives on my thinking. Specifically, about me and, with special love, this pea-size baby growing within me. Every scenario played through my head over and over after an exhaustive amount of sleepless nights pacing the hallways of her apartment building, as my mind would not stop. My thoughts, regrettably, refused to ignore my plea for solace so that I may gain a refreshing slumber. Within the storm going on in my mind, body and very soul, the answer I had been searching for came to me, whispering its solution in my ear. It turned out to be a pleasant visit, even though I spent most of it up inside my pregnant fifteen-year-old brain. With all the extra, undesignated time to think, I had an epiphany about this baby. The decision has been made. One that I needed to share with Bill.

On my first day back at school, in the cold, blustering wind chill of the Black Hills, my sophomore year began its spring semester. I was not the type to worry about my studies or future. Sometimes, it was enough for me just to get through the day. I had stormy conditions that I was navigating through. I did not have time for simple things like what I wanted out of life. Life always just seemed to happen to me. I had no time to plan for it. I was too busy cleaning up the debris from the previous storm. The encounters from this day would not be any different from those I have become accustomed to.

Bill was one year my senior, so our class schedules were irregular. We had only one class together, and it was at the end of each day: Ecology. Our teacher had basically checked out, as this was his last year of teaching before retiring on an acreage with a cabin and a small stream to fish in. So, he's become a little lazy in his final year. Although, I feel he's earned a bit of leniency, as he has been one of our most hard-working, well-liked teachers in this bizarre education center. To keep the last class of our first day back on the down low, He pops in a video and kicks up his feet onto his old, wooden desk. His chair creaks as he rocks it back and forth repeatedly while reading a newspaper article. I talk quietly to Bill about the plan that I have firmly decided on. "I want to give the baby up for adoption," I state plainly. Now, Bill wasn't crazy about the idea of adoption because that meant it would be obvious that I was pregnant. Everybody would find out that he is the father. He didn't want me to ruin the good reputation he had faked for everyone else to see. Unfortunately, all his invisible blocks tumbled down, shattering his make-believe world.

# FACING IT

My thoughts wandered through each option I had available to me as a fifteen -year-old mom. Every minute of that Christmas vacation, I was focused on what would be best for this little one developing within me. I sensed a connection with him already. I was sure I would have this baby, and with no resources to sustain him, I refused to be ignorant of my inability to raise him through his adulthood. I had completed so much research at the library, spoke with various adoption agencies on the phone, and most often and most importantly, I called out to my Lord in the agony of my breaking heart. Through pure faith, I understood this was the right decision for my baby. It is a selfless, awesome action that singularly would change the span of my baby's entire life.

Bill's character's attributes remain predictably self-preserving, and his usual narcissism is peaked as he is busted wide open with our current situation. In like manner, he altogether insisted that I have an abortion. I told him to go to hell as I grabbed a hold of my Ecology book and walked out of the class.

I was alone. That all too familiar feeling that I loathe. I had only myself to rely upon. I acted tough. But inside, I was falling apart. From that moment on, I decided to intentionally lose touch with Bill. He was neither on my side, nor did he care about this precious baby. Bill's only real concern was for himself. His self-serving attitude was one of his least likable attributes among an infinite menu list of various others.

Before the end of my first trimester, I had chosen an adoption agency out of Fresno, California. 1500 miles away from Custer. I was so certain of my decision that I contacted the agency, summing up my situation in a letter. They returned my letter with a phone call. I told them of the certainty of my decision. I think they could clearly hear the solid conviction in my voice. The agency sent me five letters and pictures, each pair being from prospective adoptive families.

I prayed to My Lord to help me make the correct choice. My prerequisites for the new adoptive family were that the couple had been married for some time, were devout Christians, and the only child they planned on having would be the one that I gave them. I wanted him to be a spoiled rotten kiddo. To have everything that I could not afford to give him as a fifteen -year-old girl. I read and reread each letter and stared endlessly at each picture of every couple needing a baby to share their love with and complete their happy family.

After much introspection and talks with My Lord, I chose The Whites, Terry and Terry. They are both teachers, Catholic, and have been married well over ten years, trying to have a child for most of their time together. After making my presumed decision, I tentatively planned to fly out and meet them at their home in

# FACING IT

California. Making the trip in early March, I exchanged my parka for a tank top upon arriving in Fresno. Terry and Terry picked us up at the airport, overwhelmingly obliging. He took our bags and placed them in their car's trunk while we girls all loaded in the air-conditioned vehicle. Nice. We drove through miles of plush neighborhoods before arriving in front of their upper- middle-class Californian home. My mom, who had accompanied me on the trip, and I were exhausted from our long flight. We had a light dinner together, just the four of us, and went to bed in the above-board accommodations. I went to sleep, dreaming of what a sweet couple they were. I had chosen right.

The next morning, during our larger -than-life breakfast the Italian wife prepared, we collectively decided to go to the beach. It was extremely windy that day, but the ocean was beautiful, and the sand felt smooth and warm under my feet. I have always had a great love and respect for the ocean. In all its vastness, it holds onto so many unseen secrets. After we all became chilled with the ocean's cold breeze blowing through our clothes, we packed up and headed to somewhere good for lunch. The husband drove us to Fisherman's Pier, a fun tourist location with rides and games, but most importantly for us right now, they had numerous eating establishments. We filled our tummies until we were comfortably overfilled, played some games and even had a profile caricature drawn of my mom and me by a street artist. I had a lot of great fun that day, but in the back of my mind, I had my secret video recording every move they made.

The next morning, Terry, the husband, took me by myself and their two sweet, old Labrador Retrievers along. Seeing him load up those aged dogs so gently, with tenderness and patience surrounding him as he performed his weekends' ritualistic task, allowed my heart to soften towards him. After obtaining his pets' necessities for our trip, we are all loaded; Terry and I in the front cab and the two dogs in the truck's camper. Those dogs could not stop jumping around in the back, bouncing from side to side, as excitement filled them for their routine weekend outing. During the drive, Terry tells me how he likes to do this every Saturday. Get up early and take his girls (the dogs) somewhere new to explore.

This Saturday, as we watched the beautiful California sunrise from the truck's windshield, I noticed us pulling into an abundant orange grove. Terry told me he knew the owner and visited here periodically with his dogs. As he tenderly helps his girls out of the back of his truck's camper, they immediately run and frolic as if they were at Disneyland. He just let them be. "I let them roam around and have fun being a dog." He tells me they will return to him when he calls their name. He and I walk along the countless rows of vibrant orange trees. They are so beautiful as the sunlight rises to give her reflection on our world. It was like peace in a visual metaphor. It was so nice to talk with Terry alone. He didn't talk about the baby unless I brought up the subject. He seemed genuinely interested in me. Asking me about school and actively listening to my answers. I could tell how he would be an awesome teacher. This is probably my favorite slice of time out of my entire visit.

Terry plucks an orange from one of the many trees within the grove. Drawing his fold-up knife from his pocket, he slices the freshly plucked fruit around its perimeter. The orange slices proudly bulge out in the warming sun of midday. The juice ran down his hand and arm. "Try a piece," he instructs me. I did. It is, by far, the best orange I have ever tasted. On the drive home, the wind gently blowing through the truck's open window, I am aware of how simple this excursion had been. Yet I had so much fun. It felt infinitely peaceful and so completely comfortable. I feel close to Terry already, and my mind has concluded that he would make an amazing father.

That same evening, Terry, the wife, a full-blooded Italian, is preparing to have her family over for dinner. People started coming and coming and coming. Everybody seemed to be in a cheerful mood. Terry's mom began asking questions about the baby. Her husband, Esmeraldo, only joked and laughed with me as he was the life of the party. I remember we were talking about the best way to die for some peculiar reason, like a heart attack or whatever, and he said, "When I die, I want to wake up dead." His thick Italian accent was apparent as he spoke. Then, his big belly from too much home-cooked Italian food would move with his laughter, making that moment even funnier and sweeter. I love the memories I carry around of them, rolling around in my head, waiting to be revisited. I left Fresno feeling good about my decision. These two were more mature than the other couples' files I had searched through to find this Mama and Papa for my baby. Their house was peaceful. They had plenty of loving family members to help care for this little one developing in my womb. Thoughts of the entire situation pinged around in my head throughout the flight back home to Custer.

Brrr...Big weather change. After our pleasant visit, we probably talked on the house phone every two to three days for several weeks. Then, something changed. About the beginning of the seventh month, when my belly had become enormous, he would kick me so hard, it would actually hurt, and I could see this little outpouching in my abdomen. With my fingers, I could gently trace his precious little heel through my belly. The days are counting down to Jordan's birth day and, coincidentally, our departure from each other. I hated Terry and Terry. They were able to care for this wonderful life inside of me, and I couldn't. He felt so real now. He felt so mine.

He made me feel like, for once in my life, I have a purpose. Soon they would be taking that awesome sense away from me. I saw them as vultures hovering over my head, wherever I was and wherever I went. They licked their lips in anticipation of the birth of this baby, then let life itself ravage my empty body. I didn't speak to them during this time, ignoring their messages on our answering machine. I know it gave them pain and made them question the entire adoption. I liked that. Let them have a taste of what I'm feeling. I know I was being mean, and I didn't care. They are taking my baby soon. About a month before the due date, I relented and called them. It was the wife. I could feel her happiness at the sound of my voice. I was purposely aloof and cold throughout our conversation. "Let her do the talking." I thought to my jaded self. I gave short answers to her many questions. She didn't ask any specifics about the baby, just wondered how I was feeling. I know she intentionally didn't push me. I could change my mind in a heartbeat, breaking theirs. Amidst the several phone calls that followed, I gradually improved my treatment towards them. I still hated them. I hated them for being them and I was a mere 15 -year-old pregnant girl in an old hick minimum wage town. Not fair. I despised the situation I was in. I loved my baby, and they would soon be taking away my love.

My labor pains began as I drifted off for a well-needed rest. The day's work had finished, and I was exhausted. I waited until midnight to wake up my mom. Custer is a small, redneck town in the Old West, so we needed to travel over an hour to get to the closest hospital. Although I went through Lamaz, learning every detail of what would happen at each progression of labor, I had no idea the pain level I would experience. Hot showers seemed to be my only friend. No epidurals in those days. It was the weekend, and the on-call doctor was not my regular doctor. My labor was not progressing, and I begged that on-call doctor to break my water, as I had learned in Lamaz that this could help speed up the labor process if you are not dilating properly. After forty hours of intense labor and no sleep for nearly two full days, I was drained. It felt like I was going to be in labor forever. Finally, the sweetest nurse entered my room and gave me a Demerol shot. It honestly didn't help the pain as much as it put me to sleep in between contractions, which at this point have become three minutes long with one minute in between. I was nearly at my breaking point. I would have taken whatever I could obtain to help this seemingly never-ending, horrendous pain.

A few minutes after eight in the morning, on Monday the 13th, after over 60 hours of intense labor, an angel walks through my hospital room door. Dr. Neu, my doctor, just came back on duty from his weekend break. He immediately assessed the situation and broke my water. Half an hour later, I was pushing. At one point during this phase, the baby's heart rate dropped to a dangerous level every time I pushed. After learning of this, Dr. Neu hastily leaves the room.

"What the hell???" My mind wanders to the worst-case scenario for why my doctor left the room so abruptly, just as I am pushing this baby out to finally meet the world. I have my feet up in stirrups, which expose my delicate for the entire room to view. But I don't even care. My modesty flew out the window at around hour ten. As this thought resonates in my head, the sweet nurse now tells me in a gentle, yet serious voice, "Now don't push."

Only a woman who has been through this can ever know the exact feeling. My body is completely ready to expel this human that has been growing inside me for so long. He is ready to come out, and my body is more than ready to be done with this laborious process. As the worry begins to take over my mind, the hospital door opens wide. Dr. Neu, with a forced smile, enters my room. As he takes his position on the stool in front of me, he announces to the nurses and me, "Let's give this one more shot." Pressing gently on my back, my sweet nurse prompts me with apprehension and pure hope, "Now, push, Liz."

Throughout my long contraction, I could hear my sweet nurse encouraging me as my eyes were squeezed tightly together, pushing with all my might. She was cheering me on. "Don't Stop. Keep on pushing, Liz." "Head's out." I can hear Dr. Neu announce to the room with exasperation. One more nearly impossible big push and he was officially born at 10:13 a.m. on August 13th, 1990. I tell the nurse to lay him on my chest as I feel the fog of hesitation in the room. He's so perfect, 8 lb. 10 oz. He was born less than two hours after Dr. Neu came on staff.

Shortly after they put him on my chest, the nurse hears a high-pitched wheezing noise that only her professional ear could catch and diagnose so readily. She quickly takes him away, saying he has a hole in his lung. Panic fills me again. "They need to take him to the NICU and put him in an oxygen-filled incubator." The sweet nurse reassures me, "It's like a pin-sized hole, and it will heal on its own in a few days. He just needs observation." Phew! …, and it lights out for my mom and me until early the next morning. Upon awakening, I immediately had a virtual instinct to see my new baby. I asked the nurse on duty to bring him to my room, as he was now already healed up and out of the NICU.

With much stalling and apprehension, the nurse relented and finally brought him to my room. I relished the time I was able to spend with him. My hand gently caresses his soft cheek. Intertwining my fingers with his and counting every little toe sneaking out of the blanket that covered him. The human touch is so vital. Sometimes I ponder whether there is a direct line between our sense of touch to our heart. He was beautiful. I loved him. When the nurse came to retrieve him from me, it concluded our time together when he was still mine. Our one and only hour of precious moments will stay with me forever. After I had composed myself, I reluctantly, yet somehow, at the same time, assuredly, made the call to the Whites. They stopped by my hospital room later that evening after already visiting with their new bouncing baby boy, whom they had decided to name "Jordan Paige White." A couple of minutes of chatter, and it was completely dead air time. Crickets. The big event was over. They would be flying home with my baby. There was nothing left to say.

I left Rapid City Regional Hospital, and my mom drove us home. Barely one word was spoken during what seemed to be the longest one-hour drive back to our house in Custer. Placing my hand over my abdomen, I felt utterly empty.

I futilely attempted to transform from adulthood back to the careless teenager I once was. Before I became pregnant and had to deal with real issues, during the time in which every decision I made had a life-changing consequence. I never cared much for school, and this year, I saw no worth in it at all. Before the start of the school year, I had requested not to be in the same classes with Bill. Upon receiving my schedule on that first day back, I found that my request had been spat upon, and I was now enrolled in each of his classes minus one. The school staff was not sympathetic to my situation at all. The principal, the secretary, and virtually all of the teachers treated me poorly.

I ended up skipping school a lot during this time, but contrary to my clipped class time, I was still pulling straight A's. Going to lunch with my friends, whom I used to hang out with regularly, proved unfulfilling. I found that I was forcing myself to make conversation. By the looks on my friends' faces, it was obvious that they sensed the awkwardness I was feeling inside. As the cool breeze of Autumn turned into winter's heavy snow, my heart felt this undeniably gnawing pain. I again placed my hand over my now empty womb. I remember giving birth, yet I had no baby to cradle in my loving arms. I couldn't shake this feeling loose. It consumed me. Although it seemed to take forever, our winter Christmas break has finally arrived. "A break from all these teenagers." I thought to myself.

Our Christmas included a trip home to Mitchell, which would have normally been entertaining and relaxing. Except, I only felt drained, depleted, done and dead inside. I faked the joy and put on my factitious smile so as not to make my family uncomfortable. We had our normal church, dinner, then the present opening. But this Christmas, as I watched my sister's little one gleefully opening all her presents, my glimpse of happiness was shadowed by my unrelenting heart pain. I truly was in the midst of grieving Jordan, yet I shared this with no one. I despised looking weak in the eyes of another. Our school break would soon be coming to an end, so we packed up my mom's tiny Horizon and drove back to Custer. Instead of the much-needed break refreshing me, it gave me too much time up inside my head, going over every detail of the past year.

Coming back to school was difficult, again experiencing the same problems as before, plus my depression was deepening. I could scarcely sit still, let alone make it through an entire day of classes. So I found myself skipping. A lot. My mom didn't care, as I felt she understood me.

One fine day, I was summoned to the principal's office. Once inside, he informed me of my bad influence on the other kids in his school. He went on to say how I made the entire student body think they could skip all the time and still pull good grades, as that is how I behaved. "I didn't know I had so much control over what other people did." was my sarcastic response as I slouched as far back as I could in my chair. My indifference enraged this sanctimonious behemoth of a man. He wanted to control me with his intimidation. I disrespectfully called him Dean, as that was his first name, instead of cordially referring to him as Mr. Keith, as all those other good students did. As I have said previously, I've always had a problem with authority figures. Especially when they misuse their authority and do not adequately perform the job that gave them this false sense of superiority. Also, he was the definition of a jackass.

As our conversation sorely deepened, Dean tried harder to bully me into submission. "Did you know I was a Navy Seal?" he proudly questioned me. He immediately followed up his question with a statement sure to frighten me. "I could kill you using one hand." He boasted as he formed his right hand into a choking motion. "Impressive, Dean. I quit." I stood up from my chair and walked out of his office for the last time.

# Chapter 4

# My Prince

Quitting school was not a bad move for me. Shortly after that critical decision, I passed my GED and had thoughts of changing up my scenery. Custer had become a bad memory that I longed to distance myself from. No one ever told me you take your memories with you.

I phoned my sister who had just moved to Sioux Falls after getting married. It boasts of being South Dakota's biggest city, with a population nearing 100,000 people. Sioux Falls is about a seven hour drive from Custer, on the very southeastern tip of our state. My call had an important purpose behind it. "I've been thinking about moving. Do you think I could stay with you guys for a while?" She answered in the affirmative. I was thankful. I didn't know if I was doing the right thing, but at least I was doing something. A few days after the phone call, I started packing my clothes and personal items, my sole possessions. It kept my mind busy, thinking about the move. It was nice to think about anything besides how much I missed Jordan.

The following morning, my mom and I said our goodbyes after having coffee together. As I slipped into the seat of my Ford Taurus, I was keenly aware that the emptiness was deepening. While driving hundreds of miles of flat plains, my mind wanders. "Am I making the right decision? I hated Custer, but it was all I had known for the last few years. Would living so far away be even harder?" I questioned every decision I had made this past tumultuous year. I blasted the radio's speakers in an attempt to drown out my thoughts. The road instantly demanded my attention, as I hit an icy spot on the highway and my car's worn tires began slipping. I quickly turn my steering wheel, while gently applying the brakes to stop my car from gravitating toward the ditch. The remainder of my drive to my new city was uneventful. I reached my sister's apartment with the directions I had written down on a piece of scratch paper I had thrown into the glove box. Sitting in the parking lot of her apartment complex, I paused in my car. To regain my composure, to put on my happy face and to be ready to fake it.

Arriving around dinner time was a plus. We all talked and ate together. It was nice. I slept on the couch and kept my belongings in the two gym bags that I had brought.

"Sunshine on my Shoulders" by John Denver played on my radio alarm clock as I awakened the next day. Determined to have a short stay at my sister's place, I procured a decent job that first full day in the big city. I always carried a city map under my car's visor because I could never find the right address anywhere, including the restaurant where I worked as a server. It paid good money and I was searching for an apartment within two weeks of moving here. I went through the newspaper, circling apartments that looked appealing. I made an appointment to look at one who's cheap rent was extremely appealing. It didn't take me long to find my perfect apartment. It couldn't have been any more adorable. It was half the upstairs of an old house. The woodwork was all original. It had a farmhouse-style kitchen sink with an old gas stove. Bear claw porcelain bathtub and built-in drawers and shelving in the bathroom. The hallway had the most quaint alcove, which I immensely enjoyed decorating. My place was coming together nicely, thanks to various garage sale finds. I am doing it on my own. I didn't need anybody and it felt empowering to be proving it.

After living a couple of months at my new apartment, I was able to save up a bit of cash. So, I decided to purchase a new pre-owned vehicle, drowning me in rent, utilities and now a car payment. "Would I have any money left over for food?" I thought to myself as I questioned my impulsive decision. I tried working two full time jobs. After several months of strict work and sleep, my body refused to go on, so I quit the second job. This left me in quite the financial dilemma. My year's lease was coming due soon and I began entertaining the idea of a roommate to help cut costs. I needed an intervention to help me keep my head above water.

After putting the word out, a former co-worker approached me about looking at apartments together. I was thrilled that she offered. I already know her and she seems normal enough. We signed a six month lease together on a decent, two bedrooms we found that was close to both our jobs. The rent is cheap. No amenities, unless you count the running water. It was nice for a while. I didn't feel so lonely all the time, because friends from my old job were always over. Every weekend, we would party until we passed out. In the morning, I would literally have to twist and turn as I would tiptoe through the sea of people sleeping on our living room floor. It was fun, for a short spell. The nearly sleepless nights and raging hangovers started to take their toll on me halfway through our six month lease. Passing out until my alarm began to buzz, awakening me at five in the morning for my 5:30 shift as a certified nursing assistant. Working in the healthcare industry, I had to work every other weekend. This style of living didn't suit me on all those Saturdays and Sundays. I futilely attempted to decrease our partying. I explained to my roommate how difficult it was for me on the weekends that I have to work. She nodded as I explained my situation to her and she seemed to be completely sympathetic. Then my weekend to work came and went, and as I tried to sleep, the partying outside my thin bedroom door ensued. Nobody could sleep with that level of noise. Sometimes I would give in and come out of my bedroom and join all of my old work friends. But eventually, I was completely worn out. This girl was not a good roommate. She was loud and irresponsible and inconsiderate and rude and messy and had ruined my outlook on roommates forever. So as soon as that 6-month lease was over, I was so far out of that situation.

I found my next apartment rather quickly. My prerequisites on any apartment was that it had four walls, a roof and was one I could afford on my puny budget. I took the first place I looked at. I was blessed to receive furniture from a friend who didn't need it anymore and gladly gave it to me free of charge. Furnished most of my small one bedroom place. I was happy to be alone again. To be able to sleep in peace, whenever I wanted. It felt really good to live without the frustration of a roommate. But there were times when I wasn't busy working or running errands. My apartment was clean and my laundry was done. I had the entire weekend off and it is 10 a.m. Saturday morning. "What the hell am I supposed to do with myself the rest of my weekend?" my mind questions me frantically. It was during these quiet times with nowhere to rush off to and no work to be done. These times were so lonely I could feel the depression sink its teeth into me. Whenever I had a moment to stop and candidly think about my life and all the moments that it has held in its fragile hands, I would find myself questioning, "What did the rest of my life hold for me?" It was during these low times I would weep over the loss of Jordan. Missing him every day broke my heart a little more. If each tear could be saved, each individual one that streamed down my face over the loss of raising my own child, I would have my own sea of tears that would challenge the vastness of the Bering Sea. I have personally found that when I am depressed, I either pout, kick and scream until I have blown out my old rock bottom and am now standing on a whole new deeper level of loneliness and despair. Or begin to ask myself different questions. Instead of asking, "Why me?", I began to ask questions like, "How can I make myself feel better inside?" Keep in mind that I am now 18, living alone in the big city of Sioux Falls. A far cry from Custer's humble population. I was working full-time at the nursing home, barely making enough money to last me through the month. I needed to make a change. I needed to be done grieving Jordan so fiercely that it consumed my days. It has been nearly three years now. I knew I needed to do something. I applied for nurses training and was accepted, pending some testing that I promptly passed. I was, for the first time in a long time, excited! A new virtuous opportunity to take this extra time off my hands, so I can put these painful thoughts and memories hidden in the back of my mind. I leaned on the Lord during this grief of mine. I would cry out to him daily. If I only knew the measure of love within my Father's heart. During this same time, I purchased my first bible while visiting my grandma in Mitchell, a one hour drive. She and I wanted to check out this new Mini Mall to have lunch, then do a little shopping. At a bookstore, I spent money I did not have on an expensive bible. Best purchase ever, hands down. I still read it to this day. The Lord is always working. I just didn't always see it.

Throughout the winter, I made several trips to Worthington, Minnesota. The town that held the college for my continuing education as a nurse. It was necessary for me to be on campus to test out of certain classes, and sign up for financial aid assistance. My core classes would begin in the spring of the following year. I had no plan on how I would survive this next year financially, and I certainly did not care. It has been a long time since I had anything to preoccupy my brain. Ultimately, it gave me something to grab ahold of. A thread of hope.

I continued my work as a CNA at the same nursing home I have been working at for the past three years. In my spare time, I would enthusiastically check out books at the library on anything to do with the practice of medicine. I couldn't tell you how many hours I studied math, anatomy and pharmacology. I would soak the information up like a sponge, taking in any knowledge my brain could comprehend.

The remainder of that cold, snowy winter went by pretty fast for me, as I kept myself constantly busy, working and learning. But then there he always was, on the back burner of my heart, pulling on my heart strings till they bust apart.

Soon the Christmas season is upon us. My mom came down for the holidays and stayed with me in my overly humble living quarters. I let her take my rickety old bed while I slept on the couch. On Christmas day, we had a lovely dinner at my sister's house. We prayed and ate. Then after the last dinner plate was removed from the festive looking dining room table, we played games, opened presents, laughed and joked with each other. It felt nice to be with some of my people once again. To feel like I belong somewhere in this gigantic world of ours. Christmas has never been a happy time for me. The entirety of the holiday season makes me feel so alone. The resonance of the holiday music playing nonstop through my radio's speakers, with all the expected cheerfulness the holiday is supposed to bring. The sappy movies on TV with commercial breaks, showing normal families gathering for a traditional Christmas dinner. It was all too much for my intensifying demise. Although, the Christmas gathering with my family did give my depression a well deserved break for a few hours. It felt like a nice cool breeze on a warm summer's day. Just a little draft to alleviate the heat of the darkness for a spell.

After Christmas time was over, my mom spent a few days with me at my miniature apartment. We would always sit and talk while we drank our morning coffee. For a couple hours, just me and her sharing what has been happening in each of our separate lives. We went to the frigid Falls and walked through its rocky terrain. One day we went shopping all day. Not my choice. Exhausting work. Before long December 31st, 1993 was upon us. My best friend, Sherry, and her husband, Larry, invited my mom and I out to a restaurant and lounge called, "Westroads". The food was delicious and the conversation was even better. I am now only 19, but have had a fake ID since I was fourteen. As a teenager, I looked much older than I actually was, so the ID never failed me and tonight was no exception. Larry was the designated driver, so my best friend and I planned on ringing in the new year inebriated. The drinks went down so smoothly that evening. Around ten o'clock, they opened up the dance floor as the band played well-known songs that everybody could sing along to, as the drinks kept coming. It wasn't long after we moved from the restaurant portion to the New Year's Eve festivities that my mom decided to call it a night, along with my sober, pregnant friend who offered her a ride home. I said my slurred goodbyes and they were off. We now had the only two unoccupied chairs in the entire place, as it was standing room only. The seats were still warm when two young gentlemen approached us, asking if the chairs were taken. My friend told them to have a seat and they promptly obliged her. I noticed the one sitting right next to me was super cute. Imagine my shock when they both ordered O'douls, the only non-alcoholic brew behind the bar. "Weirdos.", I thought. Then this same cute boy sitting next to me asks if he can bum a smoke. "Nice. Can't even bring his own cigarettes to the party. Loser." The band's melody filled the room like a thick fog of aesthetic sound. In between songs, this loser, weirdo sitting next to me begins a conversation. His voice is soft and appealing. I like it. As we sit in this overcrowded sea of faces, a lady with a basket full of roses approaches our table in hopes of a sale for herself. Just as I am ready to wave her by, this sweet boy says, "May I buy you a rose?" I choked out with surprise, "Yes." Nobody has ever done something so nice for me with knowing me for such a small slice of time. I really looked at this young man sitting beside me, as the band blasts 80s hits in the background. He has the bluest eyes that I have ever seen. Even in the darkness, I could get lost in that ocean of blue. He's wearing a dark-colored flannel shirt with cargo-style pants. I'm thinking how adorable and cuddly he looks in his flannel shirt, like a teddy bear. As he hands me the rose, I notice his hands. Large, with long fingers, big knuckles and unmanicured nails with a little bit of dirt still stuck under a few of them. A working man's hands. I like that even more. I'm beginning to think maybe this sweet, adorable boy isn't such a loser, weirdo after all. He interrupted my extremely slow thought process asking me, "Would you like to dance?" As we made our way to the dance floor, our hands intertwined. I could feel the roughness and calloused palms he carried. Hard working man. Like that best. At this point in the night, Sherry and I have completed our goal. We are both inebriated. I held him tight as we danced to The Nitty Gritty Dirt Band's "Fishing in the Dark. Being as drunk as I was, I didn't want to fall down and embarrass myself in front of this cute boy that had some spell over me already. Once we had taken our seats, we continued talking to each other. I found out his name was Tim and we exchanged contact information. "10...9...8...7...6...5...4...3...2... Happy New Year!"

I was shocked when Tim planted a New Year's Eve kiss right on my lips. Now that he had my heart's attention, we ended up talking until the bar closed up for the night. We left each other with promises of him contacting me in a couple days, after my mom would be leaving for home.

Sherry and Larry dropped me off at my apartment complex that night. Fumbling for my key in my purse, I successfully unlocked the door of my apartment and quietly made my way to the couch, so as to not wake my sleeping mother. I face planted into the couch cushions, and passed out until morning. When I awoke, Tim entered my mind, as thoughts of the previous night replayed within it. I was so hopeful that he would call. Although through my past experiences I have found that hope only brings hurt. I wished I could squelch my hope.

I moved off the couch to find my mom already awake having coffee. Early Sunday morning, we went out for breakfast, then my mom hit the road in her loaded down Horizon, headed back home to Custer. Once back at my apartment, I began cleaning to help take my mind off the fact that today is Sunday. The very day that the sweet, adorable boy from the bar promised to call. "Knock, knock." I opened my front door and was happily astonished at who was standing there. It was Tim. My heart leapt within my chest, as I invited this cute boy into my apartment. He hands me a gorgeous bouquet of fresh flowers he has brought for me. I take a deep smell of their sweet aroma before laying them on my kitchen counter, next to the single red rose he had bought for me a couple nights earlier. We sat on my couch and told each other about ourselves a bit. He told me he has been a locksmith for a few years now. I told him of my aspirations to become a nurse. I brewed us a pot of coffee, which was my only true staple at the time. Tim told me it tasted like motor oil and was almost as thick. We laughed, but continued drinking the viscous, bitterly strong coffee. Ended up spending that whole day together. The conversation just flowed with no prolonged awkward silences. I felt happy. My heart hopes that Tim is the sweet man he appears to be.

He and I spent every moment together while we weren't working. I enjoyed our time so much. He made me feel safe and that scared the hell out of me. Needing anyone is out of my comfort zone. Imagine how frightened I am already beginning to feel so close to him. I loved it and hated it at the same time. Only two weeks into his courting and he gives me the bombshell. "I love you." "I love you too." I heard my voice softly repeat back to him. It terrified me to hear those words spoken in succession. I truly could not define the "L" word, yet I say it so freely. We continued spending all of our time together. I would usually hang out with him at his own house, instead of my miniature apartment. Whenever he would stop by my place, he would bring me flowers, or groceries, or both. The first time he looked in my fridge, I had ketchup and bologna. That's it.

So Tim would periodically bring me food to ensure I was eating properly when he wasn't around. I remember him bringing me a bunch of gorgeous multi-colored tulips because I told him at an earlier date how beautiful I thought they were. He listens to me, then acts to bring me joy based on what I have said. What a concept. This guy was too good to believe. I was enjoying the ride until the day came that he would pull the rug out from underneath me. I love being with him that much. It didn't take too long for me to be spending the night at his house steadily. I noticed how nice it felt to be held before dozing off. I felt important in his arms. My life meant something because he loved me.

The South Dakota snowstorms continued blowing their strong winds with heavy snow falls through Mid-March. The thought of starting school again brought an overwhelming feeling of nervousness within me. I have invariably been in love with the idea of being a nurse. Ever since I was a little girl, taking care of my sick dolls. I would utilize my mom's nursing supplies to take temperatures, blood pressures and listen to their pretend heartbeat that only my innocent ears could hear through the long, cold stethoscope. My dreams as a little girl would soon be coming true. I would have my own live patients to care for. Albeit I was already privy to the fact that those live patients would not be as compliant as my dolls were, a lifetime ago. It felt good to be following my dream and Tim could not have been more thrilled for me. This feels weird. In the past, my significant others would hold me back to suit their own needs. And I would let them. Tim was approaching my new endeavor in life with zeal and possibilities. He was genuinely happy for me. Quite the opposite of the treatment I had become accustomed to.

Back to school days are here for me. I made the drive to Worthington Community College. Once inside, I found my appointed classroom and slid into one of the chairs within the intimidating amphitheater lecture hall. My first class was Anatomy. I hated my teacher. He had a thick accent, making taking notes in this difficult class that much more frustrating. I could tell how intelligent he was, as he would pour out all this detailed information each class without even gazing towards the book. Smart guy. My hand couldn't keep up as it futilely attempted to write down each important thought as it was spoken. An impossible task. By my third Anatomy class, Tim had the idea to purchase me a mini-recorder. He would do that. Try to fix my problems for me. Listening to his lengthy lectures on my new mini-recorder proved to be a lifesaver. Needing to grasp all these basic concepts, as they would become the backbone of the remainder of my nursing career. Upon entering our lab room, every Wednesday, the smell of formaldehyde would deluge my senses, making me puke in my mouth. We were dissecting cats for our lab project, "because they closely resemble the human body." Dr. Defanian told us. Bullshit. Translation, "The community college you are currently attending has procured these cats from an unknown source. Considering our low budget and the surplus of dead cats we have had pile in, your college administration has collectively decided to let the nursing students perform an autopsy on each cat." All I can say about that experience is that I'm glad I'm a dog person. I studied every night from my well organized notes that didn't miss a detail of the several speeches leading up to the final. Aced his anatomy class. I knew Dr. Delafanian would be proud of me. Throughout our Anatomy class together, he always called me out on the floor. He was such a perfectionist with me. If a bump on the bone was actually called a tuberosity and I would name it tubercle upon being asked, he would firmly correct me. "Whatever." was my usual response, along with the required eye roll for emphasis. "Elizabeth!" That's how he pronounced my name. "Not whatever. You need to get this right!" I grew quite fond of that man during that summer. It surprised me just how much I liked him as a human being. My next summer class was Physiology with Dr. Delfanian as my fearless professor.

My life had become quite busy. The exhilaration of my new relationship with Tim, my part-time work schedule and all those seemingly never-ending study hours kept my mind preoccupied.

But the heaviness of my baggage continued to wear me down daily. I wish so badly that someone could carry a portion of these burdens for me, lightening my heavy load. My early years take their toll on me daily. I kept my past hidden from Tim and the rest of the world, for that matter. My graphic nightmares, contributing to my sleepless nights, were a mere pebble on the mountain of memories that still haunt me and pull me back into the shadows. I have walked through the brambles, the thorns piercing my flesh as I trudge my way through the thick underbrush. The older I become, I find it's becoming harder to keep these secrets pushed down, out of anyone's sight. I learned early in life to observe what society considered to be a normal person and mimic them and everything they do. I was never my true self. Nobody would like her. I didn't like her. I was too fractured. I had so very many trust issues. I have the wall around my heart built up sturdy and tall. I was the only one that could prevent me from getting hurt. And I knew if I did end up being hurt, it was my own fault, for letting myself be so vulnerable. Deep down in my heart, I knew it would never work out between Tim and I. I wouldn't work with anyone. Sometimes people are just too broken. At least that is how I felt.

My physiology class comes to an end, taking along with it the season of summer. It was a challenging curriculum, and I aced it. I felt accomplished. Another new sensation for my mind to dissect in order to comprehend it.

Fall classes begin with a full load of credit hours. Although I am bored out of my mind during the extensively long classes, my studies are going well. I was making good friends and enjoying college life. Now that I am working much less to accommodate my nurse's training, I find that my cash flow has diminished to a slow drip. I shared this with Tim, but not to fix it. It just came up in the course of our conversation. I had barely spoken my last word and this sweet, sympathetic boy that loves me says, "Why not move in with me? We are together all the time anyways. No sense paying rent on an apartment you barely use." I was amazed at Tim's hospitality. He is in the process of showing me that love takes various forms, but I did not know it at the time. I only knew that without asking, Tim did fix it for me.

Moving day was upon us. Tim brought us special "moving day" baseball style hats to wear for the occasion. I ended up giving all my furnishings to the same friend who lent them to me. I certainly had no use for them, and I was glad to be helping my hospitable friend. We boxed up my minimalist personal items and helped my friend move the furniture onto the bed of her full ton truck. It was a smooth move and Tim made the day pleasant and at times, downright fun. He did that for me. Made me feel things that I never would have felt without him there, present with me. He gave me a break from my depression. It felt nice, but it scared me.

Moving day and every day that passed thereafter, the sum of my time was spent on Tim, school, and work. Life's show seemed to be going well for me. Our relationship was open and loving. School was a breeze. The hardest part of it was the two hour commute each day.

Then there were the days when my trust issues became a controversy between Tim and I. I worked hard to cement more bricks on that tall wall encircling my tender, wounded heart. During these times I would become enraged at him because of some phantom affair, or his spoken words that I took defensively. I was trying so hard to push him away. I didn't deserve a person to love me. Why couldn't he see through my house of mirrors into my troubled soul? I would scream, throw knick-knacks against the wall, punch and kick Tim. I didn't want to portray myself to him in this manner. It felt like an unrelenting fire inside me that I wanted to burn him with. I would yell such terrible things, hoping to hurt him so badly, that his love would turn cold. Eventually, and most certainly, from the pure exhaustion my tantrum brought, Tim would talk me down. He would grab ahold of me and hold me tight in his strong arms. He would make me feel calm once again. I immediately apologize for my dangerously damaging behavior. Each and every time he would forgive me instantly. He treated me extra nicely afterwards, totally screwing with my brain. My mind's electric system is shorting out. "Who the hell is this guy? I show him my crazy side, with my anger exploding all over him and he just forgives me?" It's too easy, too simple. What is his game plan here?" My thoughts ponder an analysis of this sweet man hugging me tightly, making me feel safe and protected and loved.

Soon after school had started, the well known snow and ice covered the interstate on my school commute. I began carpooling with one of my friends who lives close by. It makes the traveling time go by faster and saves gas money. On test days, the passenger would quiz the driver over the textbook chapter material. It was a nice set up.

Mid-October the bitter cold gave pause, as did the snow. On one of our precious few weekends off together, Tim and I packed up a picnic and headed for Newton Hills State Park, only a half hour drive away. We got lost hiking the many winding trails around the hills of the beautiful, green, tree-filled park. As the warmth of the sunshine shone on my face, I took Tim's hand in mine, interlocking our fingers. It was a delightful day, and spending it with this new love of mine only made it that much sweeter. We walked around the thin, poorly groomed trails up and down the big hills, hand in hand. After a couple hours of hiking, we found our way back to the car, where our picnic lunch lay inside. We ravenously ate our sandwiches and chips, as we sat at the worn, wooden picnic table, deep in conversation. Tim tells me of this cool lookout that they have built within the state park. "If you climb the stairs all the way to the top, you can see for miles." We both agreed it would be a good ending to a great day. With each stair, our progress became slower, but we were determined to make it to the top of the lookout. So, we trampled on. One step at a time. "You were right, honey." I said to

Tim. "I can see for miles." I was awestruck at its beauty. Most of the trees are evergreens, so the hills are still alive and deep green in color. I can see the next town over that's in close proximity to the state park. After the beauty eludes me, I notice that Tim is not beside me. I turn around in search of him. My heartbeat quickens, as shock fills my body. There is this sweet, cute boy, in the dark flannel shirt, kneeling before me with a sparkly ring in his hand. "Elizabeth, will you marry me?" He slips the ring on my finger. As I bend down to kneel beside him, I whisper, "Yes." in his ear. We embraced for a long time, but it could never have been long enough. My cup was full and my heart surrendered to the completeness it perceived. We stayed at Newton Hills for a while longer, until our toes and noses were too cold to go on. We walked, or rather skipped, along the path. Our hands clasped together. Being with my now Fiancé, I feel whole. After we watched the sunset, our legs made their way to our vehicle. The car's heater warms my skin. It feels good to unthaw our numb legs and frozen toes. We both felt vitalized and enthused about our news. We couldn't just go home after something monumental like this had occurred in our life. I have a deep seeded need to share my amazing news with somebody.

We decided to go to my sister's since she was the only family I had in town. I couldn't wait to share my unbelievable news. My excitement was intoxicating. As I placed my hand in my sister's for her to properly examine the engagement ring, I noticed how perfect it looked on my finger, like it was always meant to be there. A couple bricks fell off that wall around my heart. It felt weird. It had never happened before.

School studies took up a huge chunk of my time in the upcoming months. I felt confident as I began to put my nursing skills to practice in clinical settings at various healthcare facilities in the area. Springtime flowers were now in full bloom and I was getting ready for my graduation in May, while in the midst of planning our wedding, which was set for mid-October of this year. So far that is all we have accomplished in planning our wedding. Setting the date.

I graduated with a full cap and gown. A first for me. I stayed the course. I had accomplished my goal, with honors. As they announced my name, I took center stage to shake hands and receive my diploma. I felt driven.

Finding employment was easy. I simply took my CNA shoes off and slipped into my new, bright, white LPN shoes at the same nursing home I've been working at for years now.

Tim and I are both head over heels in love and eagerly anticipating our wedding. We are both working full time and have so much to do to plan for our big day. Tim has a huge family. We sent out over 200 invitations! At this time, Tim is Catholic, so I need to complete the RCIA process to become Catholic. This is a requirement so that we can be married in the church he grew up in.

# FACING IT

The confirmation takes several hours each week at a class in the fellowship hall of St. Michael's Church. It was good for me. Gave my soul a refreshing Spring rain, where a seedling is growing slowly as I've been tending to it throughout my lifespan. The seed was planted by God in my heart, but I am not a good gardener.

I have never had, nor much cared for the traditional life, and this wedding would show that through and through. I wasn't the type of little girl who dreamed of her wedding day; I was much too busy futilely hiding from the darkness of the shadows. I didn't care about the service, or the food, the entertainment, or the traditional guest book. I simply wanted to be married to the sweet, adorable boy I met not that long ago. My heart longed to be Tim's forever bride. Our venue was the VFW, which does not exactly scream elegance. So I threw one hundred dollars at my best friend Sherry and told her to make this place look like the Hilton. My brother, Mike, volunteered to be the photographer, as he majored in that very subject in college. Grabbed my dress and veil off the clearance rack at some fancy boutique, and set up the menu with the cook at the VFW. Just in the nic' of time, we're done. I think. I'm hoping we've covered all our bases with the preparations because out of town family and friends will be traveling here soon.

Most importantly for me, my entire family made it to Sioux Falls. My two brothers flew in from out of town. Mike and his wife from Michigan and Sean from Washington. My sister Michelle and her entire family made the long drive from Indiana. My mom came up from Custer, stopping by Mitchell to pick up my Grandma. My now pregnant sister, Monica, and her family, as you know, already live here. My tribe has arrived. Although small in number, we always leave a big impression. The night before our big day my entire family got wasted at a honky tonk bar called, "Borrowed Bucks Roadhouse". My pregnant sister came out with us for a long while before she retired for the night, sober of course. We yell back and forth to each other over the music blasting from their sound system. We rocked that country dance floor. We hugged and cried. We smiled and laughed so hard our guts would hurt. It is the most fun I have ever had with all my adult siblings.

That night, I shared a room with one of my friends from college in the same hotel that my family was staying at. Once we all got back from the bar, we crashed, hard. The next morning, I had an early morning hair appointment. Pictures were tentatively scheduled for noon, with the wedding beginning at 2 o'clock. I rolled myself out of bed. The impact of the floor helped awaken me. I splashed some water on my face and was out the door. As my friend, Dana, curled and styled my long, dark brown locks of hair, I ate an entire roll of Tums. No hangover could make me regret the time I had with my people last night. I grab hold of these precious slices of time, like a lifeline, and I keep them in the forefront of my mind. Priceless time, a nonrenewable resource, whether you make use of it or not.

A fine commodity that can never be replaced. It cannot be bought, sold or trade. It cannot be given or received from another. You have the time the Good Lord gives to you daily and we all know how fast it travels by us. Dana did an amazing job on my hair. The way she made the curls envelop my face, it looks so beautiful, so romantic, so feminine. She told me she'd be seeing me at the wedding, and I was on my way to the church to put on my make-up and slip into my wedding dress.

Being ready a little early, I decided to have a cigarette before I went out to the sanctuary for pictures. I propped the back door of the church building open, so it wouldn't lock me out and went outside for a smoke. I have my hair done and my long sequined veil is intact. I have applied my make-up and am wearing my long, white wedding gown. My sneaky brother Mike captures this silent moment in time with a black and white photo. Beautiful, sunny October day with temperatures in the 60s. Gorgeous bride waiting for her groom, with hair and make-up perfect, white gown and veil moving with the gentle breeze. And in her hand, a lit cigarette. As I take a drag and exhale, smoke encompasses the camera lens. "Click." Frozen in time forever. One of my favorites. The photo embodies who I am.

It was my turn at bat, but I wasn't alone. As we walked down the aisle, arm in arm, my two valiant brothers on each side of me, I felt happy and loved. Nervous, but certain. Mike could not have looked more proud and Sean had tears rolling down his face as they gave their baby sister away to her groom that had been awaiting her arrival. Another moment in time that I will keep close to my heart till the end of my days. As our arms slipped apart, I turned and hugged each one of my brothers. I then placed my hand in the rugged hand of my sweet groom.

We have written our own vows to each other, which was my idea wholly. Tim obliged me, as he often does. As we lit our unity candle, handcrafted by us, I finally had a chance to look at all our family and friends that took time to attend our wedding. Touching. As the ceremony is almost through, the priest announces, "You may kiss the bride." Just like the night we met, Tim surprises me again. Not with the kiss I was expecting, but a much longer, more romantic kiss. As the priest announces, "I now present you with Mr. and Mrs. Walter." Once the kiss had ended, we walked back down the aisle, facing the crowd. I once again see all the faces, most of them foreign to me now. Although each one will affect my life from this point forward. I will become closely connected to so many of these people, because of the connection Tim and I had that fateful night nearly two years ago. I feel so in love. So excited. So exhausted. So married.

After the long ceremony, Tim's best man chauffeured us around in my decorated, white Chevy Cavalier. Tim and I were both famished. We went through the Burger King drive thru, and when all the employees saw we were newly married, they gave us our food at no cost. Non-traditional start to an untraditional marriage. Funny memory. It seems peculiar at times, these random memories we hold onto so dear.

Arriving at our reception hall, I see my best friend has not failed me. She has gone above and beyond what I asked her to do on an extremely low budget. Sherry and Larry have made this dull, drab VFW look better than the Hilton. I was awed at the transformation and grateful for all the work they have put into this unbelievable feat. It was an unforgettable night filled with music from a live band supplied by the VFW, that we lovingly referred to as "The Old Cowboys." Our friend, who was a Billy Ray Cyrus look alike in Las Vegas even took the mic for a few songs, including the crowd favorite, "Achy Breaky Heart." While Tim took a break to smoke a hand-rolled cigar with his buddies, I went into the bathroom. Found a few female members of my clan already there, smoking weed. I could smell the skunkiness of it as I watched the thick smoke pour out my mouth. I took a couple of hits. I didn't feel it though. I was already on an awesome natural high. Felt like I was flying and I didn't want my feet to ever touch the floor. No drug could have made me feel any higher. The entire reception is a total blur. Tim introduced me to so many of his people. Matching names with faces that I knew I wouldn't remember, at least not from this dim-lit, hazy night's inauguration. I didn't have to introduce Tim to anybody. He already knew all of my guests. I was genuinely grateful for all my friends that showed up from college and work. It added numbers to my small inner circle of people. Tipped the scales in my favor a bit, or at least got my side off the ground. His 200 to my 50. I was glad to be marrying into a large family. It made me feel like I was a part of something much bigger than myself.

We ate, drank and were merry. We auctioned off my garter to Uncle Frank, one of the few faces I would remember. He bought my garter for $100. A huge chunk of change in the mid-90s. A jaw dropping amount of money to give for a $2 garter. Memories. After the garter auction, we all hung out and chatted amongst ourselves while some of us let loose on the dance floor. Everybody was visiting with each other, having a magnificent time together. In the midst of the smoke, the music and the laughter, my new husband grabbed ahold of my hand and we snuck out of our own reception to go to our hotel room that we reserved for our honeymoon night. Sweet dreams.

That next morning, we all came together one last time for a morning brunch and present opening for the new bride and groom. Tim's parents hosted the coming together of both families at their humble home. It was nice having the immediate family members from both sides together in a more intimate and less formal setting. After the last present was opened and we had taken our last sip of freshly brewed coffee, my family and I stepped outside to give each other hugs while saying our tear-filled goodbyes. We promised each other we'd all get together real soon. Empty promises. People make so many empty promises. Maybe it's to avoid the harshness of speaking the truth. Why not simply allow silence to fill the air? Awkward! Instead, we fill that empty air space with our many empty words that build up to more empty promises. I have made so many in my short 21 years on this planet. Forever wishing I would have fulfilled most of them. But that is one thing that you can never get back: time after it has passed.

We left his parents' home en route to Savannah, Georgia. We had previously mapped out our route to our honeymoon destination, which was 1400 miles ahead of us. Driving that far after just getting married is not conducive to love and passion, but instead is replaced with boredom and contempt. Being together in the car, talking over the things we would see and do once in Savannah was exhilarating. Once our words were depleted, I read aloud our wedding cards to Tim as he drove. There were so many. I enjoyed slipping my finger under each individual envelope, pulling it open and often, ripping the entire envelope apart. After reading through the last card, I slouched down in my reclined seat to take a nap. Upon awakening, I read my book and Tim and I talked for a spell. He turned on the radio. I was exhausted. I think Tim is too. It was not fun. We did not talk endlessly like I had previously pictured in my head. I was completely ready to get out of this car. Thank goodness. We are stopping to sleep for the night.

Day two of driving. We stop to get something to eat for breakfast after a couple of hours on the road. After being seated by our waitress, I became enraged because I think my new husband is being too nice to her. Jealous much? In my head, I figured Tim married me until the next pretty girl came along. My trust issues are alive and well. Even on my honeymoon. I actually took the keys and drove our car, alone, back on the interstate going the opposite direction towards Sioux Falls. As I sped along, my thoughts were zooming wild pictures through my brain. Each scenario being worse than the last. I drove about forty miles out before my thoughts turned to that sweet boy in the dark flannel shirt, sitting in the restaurant booth that I had just left him in. My heart sank, "What am I doing?" I took the next exit to turn around and drive the forty miles back to the restaurant. I, of course, was apologetic, yet defensive. He hugged me. "I'm just glad you came back." Several bricks fall from the wall within my chest. I'm not sure I like that. I've worked so hard to build it. This sweet boy is becoming my kryptonite. After the restaurant incident, the road flows under our wheels as they hum down the interstate, finally arriving at our hotel in Savannah Georgia. We were both exhausted, yet invigorated.

We completely enjoyed the time we spent together as newlyweds on our honeymoon. We sat in the sun, by the pool, in the perfect 80 degree heat. We watched the random street performers, which quickly became our favorite attraction. The old men jazzed it up on the riverside, as their harmonious melody filled the warm air of the Georgia night. The unicyclist who would juggle anything, including knives. Scary, but entertaining nonetheless. We walked hand in hand on the boardwalk, watching the big cargo ships pass by as several cranes swooped overhead in search of dinner. We were enveloped with one another's love. Each moment was like a dazzling jewel, kept in the treasure box of my heart forever. Our time went by way too fast, as good times often do. As we sat at a riverside bench, we reminisced as we contemplated our long car trip back home.

# Chapter 5
# Faking It

Our trip back home was not nearly as nerve wracking. We were more laid back and relaxed from our four days spent soaking up Savannah's sun together.

Now it was back to life, back to reality. I've hidden the fact that this will be a whole new reality for me. Sanity doesn't feel quite right when I've grown up with pure insanity. That first year of marriage was quite an adjustment for me. I moved out over a dozen times, whether the sun was blazing hot or it was snowing sideways. I was leaving Tim; come hell or high water. Packed up all my stuff and with a loaded down white Chevy Cavalier, I would peel out of the driveway in my undeniable, uncontrollable anger. After driving around a while, I realized I had nowhere to go. My adrenaline has slowed down, enabling me to feel the full impact and pure guilt from another outburst. I would always return home, tail tucked between my legs. Tim, being the steady one in our relationship, would say to me, "I'm just glad you are home safe." At times forgiveness was not spoken, merely implied. I wished I could be a normal bride. My defenses were fully loaded at all times. My trust issues were insatiable. Reminds me of my husband's forgiveness.

During the summer of the following year, amidst the chaos and forgiveness, the freshly budding love and the noise of the outside world, Tim and I found out we were pregnant. We had both wanted children right away, and seeing that positive sign on the pregnancy test brought us profound joy. The next morning that joy was accompanied by morning sickness. I had Saltines and Sprite at my bedside, so I could eat a few before sitting up. A nifty trick I read in one of my many pregnancy and child-rearing books. It rarely worked for me. Every morning, without fail, I would get sick several times. After the first trimester, the sickness dissipated until it was replaced by heartburn. Small discomforts in the grand scheme of things. I love being able to feel this baby of ours moving within her nine-month living quarters. She made me fully aware of her presence whenever she had hiccups or did aerobics within my belly. I was overjoyed to be pregnant and my distinctive glow showed through. It felt so wonderful as Tim would place his rough hand over my belly in hopes of feeling the baby kick. He would patiently wait and "kick". Those baby blues would light up, as would his entire face. We were both so completely in love with her. God would continue to form her within me, knitting her organs and systems together so that they work according to his design. Stitching unique DNA to each of her tiny cells, which daily grow in number by the millions.

I continued to work until my due date. After I had clocked out from my last day of work, I carefully sat in my white Chevy Cavalier. It has become harder to drive because if I put my seat back far enough to accommodate my swollen belly, my feet can't reach the pedals. "Appears like you are going to have to endure being squished for the ride home, little one," I thought to my sweet baby as I pulled the seat forward and drove home. As I arrive home from my last day of work, I am eager to see the baby's room. While Tim and I were talking before I left this morning, he informed me of his plans to paint the walls some mild shade of yellow. Imagine my displeasure at the surprise I walked into. All day, I've been anxiously awaiting to see his progress, only to find he has stripped the walls he was supposed to paint yellow, right down to their framing. He ripped up the carpeting, too, unveiling the original hardwood underneath. He explains to me how he has ordered new windows and plans to sand and refinish the floor to its original luster and...

I lost track of his many words as I thought of how I would be giving birth any day, and we had no room for the baby. Because my sweet, unconventional husband has waited till this point in the pregnancy to entirely gut the baby's room. I had plans on fulfilling my nesting instincts during this period of time while we perseveringly waited for our baby's readiness to meet her new world. I had prepared to assemble her crib and hang up all the cute clothes we received at our baby shower. I would stock up the diapers and wipes, maybe even hang a picture or two on the freshly painted yellow walls of her room. Instead, I was looking at wall studs, a shabby wood floor and old windows with construction debris strewn about the room. He explained to me how he entered her room with every intention of simply painting the walls. Looking around, he wondered how much better he could make this room for our new baby. He went downstairs to grab his sledgehammer and safety glasses, and "It just kind of got away from me." he says sheepishly. I make fun of him for taking away my ability to nest properly. I actually didn't mind at all. It would be nice to have the bedroom he would eventually transform this riddled mess into.

I feel the intense pain just as I'm drifting off to sleep. Tim grabbed our "go" bags, and we were off to the hospital. I was able to receive an epidural after I had dilated to a four, which changed the birthing process altogether. After receiving the pain block, I was able to sit up in bed and talk to the many visitors I had in my room. Everyone was present in great anticipation for the birth of our baby. We never did find out the gender. Boy or girl, it made no difference to us, and we both wanted it to be held in secrecy until the birth. After my doctor broke my water, things progressed rapidly, and before long, it was time. I pushed over and over again with every ounce of strength I had left in me. Then I heard the most magnificent sound. My baby's first cry. "It's a girl!" my doctor exclaims. Savannah was officially born at 2:45 pm on April 11,1997. The nurse laid her on my chest, and I finally met this miniature human who has had my heart from the start. My index finger brushes her cheek, and as my eyes meet hers, I notice her remarkably long eyelashes. She is so gorgeous and looks just like her daddy. If she looked up, her eyelashes would touch her faint eyebrow. My hand moves down to caress her tiny fingers. Her skin is so soft. She is completely perfect, and she is all ours. I felt full of pure, unconditional love for this precious little baby girl.

She was absolutely amazed at this new world she has embarked on. Her eyes grew wide as she would curiously inspect her surroundings. I do not think she even blinked until she finally fell asleep in my arms around four in the morning. How could we know that this little eight-pound bundle would change our world in some way with each decision she would ever make. From this point on, we will be walking beside her when she needs comfort, in front of her when there's danger ahead and behind her when she's afraid she may fall.

Tim woke up and walked towards our hospital room door to prevent a nurse from entering who wanted to give Savannah "a quick hearing test." I listened to her attempt to persuade him to allow her entrance, but he vehemently stopped her passage at the door's threshold. We were both utterly exhausted. Both of us have been awake for well over forty hours. Nothing could come between us and sleep except this precious little bundle asleep in my arms, oblivious to all the commotion. This has become my new, magnificent reality. Tim and me and this undeniably beautiful baby make three.

# FACING IT

We had an army of family and friends visiting to see our new baby girl, Savannah. Everyone was in awe of her. How aware she was of every sight and how cuddly she was, as each guest insisted on holding her for a bit. I loved that my girl had so many people. She has two families that absolutely adore her and will remain a part of her life forever. I am grateful that she is so enveloped by love.

While being discharged from the hospital a couple of days later, we found ourselves in the midst of a South Dakota full-fledged blizzard.

Attempting to be that perfect mom from the beginning, I had brought a snowsuit for a "just in case" scenario. Tim pulled our vehicle around to the front door of the hospital. Our nurse brought me, holding our new bundle of joy, to meet him in the courtesy of a wheelchair.

This is it. We are parents. On our way home with this new life that God has entrusted us with. He will continue to uplift us through each stage of her many days to come. Upon entering our mudroom, it felt good to shrug off the frigid chill from outside. Albeit, more importantly, to bring our new little one inside, where we could protect her from the cold and snow. As I removed the thick woven blanket covering Savannah's car seat, I saw her again. Wide awake, of course. As I became lost within the ocean in her eyes, I was dumbfounded at how much I loved her. She could do no wrong.

Nothing she would ever do could ever add or subtract an ounce of love I have for her. Maybe that's why God allowed me to be a mom. He was showing me what a small crumb of His love feels like. It is undeniable and absolute. Nothing can ever change the measure of love He gives us. It was a lesson He would be teaching me throughout this big adventure we all call life. I vowed at that moment to always care for and protect her. Ready to catch any fiery dart before it is even within her range, to keep her safe from everything…and everyone.

In the course of our first year with Baby Bannah, as her two-year-old cousin so lovingly referred to her as we all transitioned together. Tim and I are changing our circadian rhythm, enjoying being able to function on one of two things: either little sleep or no sleep at all. Savannah is enjoying the less cramped living quarters, as well as discovering her fingers and toes.

I wanted so badly to be that white picket fence, apron-wearing, pie-baking, "How was your day, honey?" kind of mom and look great while doing it. And I was that person for a while. "I am hopelessly lost." I would think to myself often, but I dared tell no one. This secret is staying hidden within me. I read a lot of baby-rearing books during my maternity leave. If the book couldn't advise me on an inquiry, improvisation became the answer until I could get advice from a more experienced mom.

# FACING IT

I knew Savannah would be an only child because I loved her so much. I felt there was no more room in my heart for another child, as she had already filled it up to the brim with the love I had for her. As a mom, I am learning that a heart becomes full not from love received but rather from the love given to another. And mine was bursting at the seams. Tim is head over heels in love with her. From the first time he laid eyes on her, his whole face lit up. He would often snag her from my arms to hold her himself. Safe and cozy, Savannah would lie comfortably at peace in his arms. He is such a proud papa.

I stayed home for eight weeks before returning to work. I hated going back and leaving my Savannah with another person to care for her. Dealing with several daycare issues did not ease my anxiety over the situation. The first daycare we tried, the lady was really sweet. But when I would pick up Savannah after I got off work, I could count the thirty kids she was caring for. One of them being my precious girl. "Oh, no. This will not do." I assured myself. We handled this first fiasco with two parts: I went down to part-time at my work, and we changed babysitters to one that a friend had suggested. We did not upgrade with this choice. This lady was not sweet. Barely pleasant most times. She had the right number of kids in her daycare, but she did not truly care for any of them. One afternoon, I received a phone call from her while I was at work. Her voice, on the other side, seemed frantic. "Your baby has been crying ever since your husband dropped her off. She won't stop." I'll be right there." as I slammed the phone down onto the receiver. Worry consumed me on the drive over to her daycare. Information about shaken baby syndrome was rolling around in my now frantic, fearful thoughts. Everything with Savannah ended up being okay once she saw her mom. I think we dodged a bullet getting our baby out of that daycare when we did. Tim and I discussed our current situation that evening until we came up with a solution. It was a short discussion, as we were both on the same page. The next day at work, I gave my two-week written notice. The Director of Nursing begged me to reconsider. For me, the decision had already been chiseled in stone. I finished my part-time job while my family helped care for Savannah.

My life took a drastic change as I stepped out of my bright white nursing shoes and into my stay-at-home mom tennis shoes. I have always been very particular regarding my job performance and took on this endeavor with the same zeal and perfectionism. My eight-hour nursing shifts had ended, and my 24-hour shift as a mom and a wife had just begun. Although, this time, I loved my boss, Savannah. I did anything I could to save money for us since Tim was now the sole breadwinner for our family. I made fresh baby food with various fruits and vegetables instead of buying the expensive small jars at the store that are also full of preservatives. I also homemade her baby wipes from a recipe handed down from a good friend. I would cook nearly palatable meals and have dinner ready when Tim got off work. This all seemed to be working for me, for us.

"Keep on mimicking the other sunscreen-slathering, tissue-carrying, sunhats-required type of moms." I told myself. The ones that play with their kids in the park while visiting with the other random parents. I follow the instructions the books have given me on raising an infant, trying to fit in as a new mom our first time at the park. Playing with Savannah on the swings, giving the tiny pushes that make her giggle. Which makes me smile and genuinely laugh along with her. Everybody at the park that day thought I was a regular, normal mom. If only they could have heard the silent dialogue in my head. "You are not good enough. Try harder, you are failing. Do better!" The constant chatter between my two ears makes me feel inept as a mother, a wife and a basic human being. I am filled with shame and guilt. I do not know the definition of "normal," so it is hard for me to act like it. The other moms are discussing mom things with me, and I try to act natural. Like this is who I really am. But I can only fake it for so long before my charade will inevitably end in disaster.

In October of that following year, we lost my grandma to colon cancer. She cared for me often as a child, sometimes all five of us kids. What a saint she is to have put up with all of our shenanigans. Our love for one another was quite mutual. So as she lay semi-conscious in a nursing home bed, I was right by her side. I would swab her mouth to keep it from drying out as it was constantly open now. Her breathing became more shallow and would make a rattling sound with every breath. My sister Michelle and I were there for the last few days together. One night as she cried out something inaudible, I crawled up into the hospital bed and held her emaciated body with my strong arms, like she would do for me as a child. I have found that the human touch brings peace to those in any kind of pain. As I watched her suffering, I prayed that God would take her. Each of her words had already been spoken, and the cancer had ravaged her body. I cradled my grandma in my arms to comfort her. Early the next morning, we could sense a change in her breathing. She had periods of apnea, and the rattling sound had increased its volume. Even though I was sending prayers to God to end her suffering, as I saw my grandma breathe her last, I was shocked and inconsolable. It befuddles me how the mind and heart work so differently. My mind knew it was time for her to be with the Lord, but my grief-filled heart would not accept it.

Later that same year, a cousin that I had grown close to as an adult was diagnosed with brain cancer at the young age of forty. The doctors performed surgery three times before they told her there was nothing else they could do and sent her to live in a nursing home for her last days. More sadness. My cousin had a tumultuous life, and now she lay in a nursing home, waiting to die. It brought me utter despair for her and her teenage daughter. With each visit, I saw her deteriorating, and my sadness would deepen. I honestly didn't know what to do with this thick blanket of intense emotions. I wanted to purge myself of all the grief, the loss, and frustration. I think the bible has the right way to deal with grief. Sitting in the dirt for days while I tear at my clothes. I toss dust in the air, and as it falls back to the earth, a portion of it fills my long hair and covers my face. My loud cry out to my Lord can be heard to the heavens. But with advancements, we fall backwards into this stoic, detached, matter-of-fact grief. Bereavement that is too clean. I have found that humans do not prefer to get dirty, instead, we wrap things up in a pretty bow and say, "Whala!" Grief is over. But it never is.

As the winter snows ring in the new year, Tim and I continue to be in love with each other and our Baby Bannah. He has lessened the power of grief's uppercut because He is in the ring with me. He listens to my troubles endlessly while holding me in his strong arms, safe and protected.

That February, I received a flier in the mail regarding fundraising for cancer opportunities. Thinking this may help in some small way, I attended that first informational meeting. During this session, I learned it is a fundraiser that ends with the participant running a marathon. I sign up for this worthy cause, committing my precious time to this necessary grief purge. I would rarely cry during this time of "my perfect self." My sadness was unrecognizable to others and was swept under the rug with all the dust of my past. That same evening, they gave us a training schedule. It contained a program with shorter runs during the week, a long run on Saturday and a day of rest for Sunday. As I left the meeting and was driving home, I felt good about my decision. I was doing something. Isn't that what life is? One step at a time down the path that is rolled out before us. One decision, one choice to act or retreat, all combined to shape our life.

Returning home, Tim was happy that I was becoming involved in this outreach. He bought me a large bike stroller for my daily runs with Savannah. It had so much room, and it was like her little fort on wheels. Totally sweet of him to support me in all my endeavors. He saw through my stoic facade. I showed him my tears. Looking back now, I guess I sort of trusted him at this point, at least with the surface-level stuff. Which, for me, was progress.

A couple of days into my training, I was telling my sister, Monica, about what I was doing. Being a fitness freak herself, she instantly wanted on board. I introduced her to the director of the program. She gave each of us purple running tank tops and instructed us to print the names of who we are running for on the back. My sister and I decided we would do the weekday runs by ourselves and do the long run on Saturday together. Five days a week, I would complete my short runs alone. Savannah would sit on a soft pillow in her larger-than-usual stroller space, tucked safely inside with her sippy cup, a variety of snack options, her colors and other crafting materials, dollies, and of utmost importance, the stuffed teddy bear that she would snuggle safely in her arms. She truly enjoyed those runs with me. Seeing nature at its finest from the comfort of her little hideout, pacing along the trails. On Saturdays, Monica and I would complete our long, arduous runs together. We would then usually puke together once we stopped. I learned quickly that long runs do not do my digestive system any favors. I visited Karen often during this time. I wanted to keep her involved in what I was doing. I would give her updates on our fundraising and training progress. I would try to make her laugh or at least smile. The schedule we were following gave our bruised bodies one week to heal before we left for the marathon. My cousin died this week. She had run the race, fought the good fight, and now she was in the midst of peace and love. Holding hands with my grandma in heaven. My heart broke a little more. Losing her right before our race is like a hard punch to the gut. It hurts so much all you can do is fall to the ground in a heap.

Soon it was our time to leave. The Cancer Society flew us out to San Diego on their dime. We had managed to raise over $10,000.00 together. The generosity of people is overwhelming. September 23rd, 1999, arrived. My sister and I pin each other's racing numbers on our shirts that have "I am running for Grandma and Karen" printed on the back. I was amazed by the sheer number of people that were participating in this, the first-ever "Rock n' Roll" marathon. As the starter's pistol rang, we were off. A lot of the people sprinted straight away from the ring of the shot. We started out slow. A fast walk at first, just waiting for the crowd to thin out a bit so we have room to move. I was keeping pace with my sister pretty steadily until I hit that wall at mile twenty and wanted to quit running. My sister will not allow it. She took my hand in hers, and I ran that last 6.2 emotional miles holding my sister's angelic hand. My thoughts went to Karen and grandma. Each moment I remember holds a different emotion, filling my heart with warmth and tenderness. With one mile left to go, my legs refused to go any further. They wanted me to stop where I stood and pour cement in them, so they would never have to move again. Retire. Meet other former marathon legs. My thoughts were going goofy with exhaustive delirium. My thighs burn from the hot fire within. My shins feel like they have been beaten with a board repeatedly. My gut has been cramping for a while and is now wrenching and churning as my nausea increases. I was depleted. Then, there it was. The finish line! Straight ahead, about a city's block worth of asphalt left to pound with my poor, hurting, bloody feet. It hurts each time one of my feet touches the ground. The marathon's photographer took an emotion-filled picture of my sister and I as we crossed that finish line, hands clasped together and raised high in the air. Wonderful memory. I knew it was the dear Lord that had carried me this far, and it was pure faith that brought those beaten-up legs across that finish line. I could sense my grandma and Karen wink at us from heaven. We had fought a good fight. We have finished our race. A marathon volunteer wrapped me in a runner's blanket, which is basically a reflective foil like material. After putting my body through that much punishment, it was going into shock. Instead of feeling the sweltering hot 90-degree California day, I was chilled to the bone. My body shook uncontrollably. My knees stopped bending, and I resembled the tin man when I walked. My sister felt the same way and as we watched, we saw everyone that was crossing that finish line was experiencing the same phenomenon. I rehydrated, and after quite a long while, my pain-filled knees started to bend, allowing me to walk naturally again. This phenomenon made me correlate my physical body to my psyche. I can only take so much pounding, hurting, burning pain until I stop. With that pause, something within me thinks, "I will not take this any longer," and I go into shock. Nobody has told me what to do with this emotional shock.

That night the marathon hosted a gigantic block party for all of us, filling our stomachs with carbs and our ears with music from "Hootie and the Blowfish." I was on a definite runner's high. An anomaly occurred when I crossed that finish line, accomplishing my goal. Something ridiculously purging. It is an unexplainable, incredibly miraculous healing. A lot of processing went through my mind amidst those hundreds of miles of pavement-pounding training.

The next afternoon we flew home with our marathon medals around our necks as a tangible souvenir of the phenomenal experience life just handed us.

The rest of 1999 goes on without a hitch, and Y2K does not shut down the world as we know it.

Sometime in mid-March, my mother-in-law, Betty, had won a trip to New York, and she asked me to come along. I was thrilled to be offered the opportunity to explore The Big Apple with her. Several days before we left, I noticed that I was late and promptly took a pregnancy test. "Wait, am I reading this right? Are we? Could we actually be? Pregnant?!?"

Our four-day trip to New York was a whirlwind of Broadway shows, Little China, trolley tours, The Statue of Liberty and Ellis Island. We took in all the regular tourist attractions the big city has to offer. We hardly slept because we wanted to take everything in and feel the rhythmic heartbeat of the city within our bones. We ate our breakfast from a food truck each morning like a true New Yorker would. One of our excursions involved a long elevator ride through the building's many floors, then an escalator trip to the very top of The World Trade Center. The view was magnificent. I could see the entirety of New York City, including its three gargantuan bridges. I felt mystified at the splendor of the view, as my eyes were busy taking mental pictures. Several other tall buildings attempted to reach the height of The World Trade Center in their rivalry. Betty and I sat on a bench, comfortably soaking it all in. We watched all the other tourists walking around the perimeter of the platform we were on. The gentle breeze that blew through our hair chilled us like a strong gust of northern wind had wafted through. We sat in silence at the pure magnificence of the tall towering building and the spectacular view it gave us. Who could have known what would be happening mere months from now? Such a travesty. Thank goodness God gives us time in small doses. No one could take all the tragedies their life will hold all at once. The instantaneous emotions might make our vulnerable heart want to give up and stop its rhythmic beating. God always knows what he is doing. He created us and breathed His breath of life into us. I trust He knows what He is doing with my life.

One evening, Betty contacted our cousin and her husband, who live in 'the city so nice, they named it twice'. They treated us to dinner at a fancy Italian restaurant, where they served everything family-style. It was a beautiful dinner. After we had finished eating, they let me pick the dessert. It was the first time I have experienced tiramisu. It tasted so undeniably sweet. A much different sweetness than the Little Debbie Snacks I'm accustomed to. It's funny how thinking back to the deliciousness of that coffee-based dessert not only makes my mouth water but also brings me back to that quaint, dimly lit Italian restaurant and the time I shared with my newly found cousins. I'm learning that, at times, it's good to remember.

After we had left the restaurant with full bellies and full hearts, the husband insisted that it's not a true New York visit until we had experienced their transportation system. He quickly flagged a cab, and as we three girls piled in the back seat, he took the front. It was an interesting ride, a pretty stereotypical New York cabbie. On the husband's guidance, the cab driver takes us to this sculpture-filled park. Some of those art sculptures were so large you could stand within them. We snapped a few pictures and took the subway back towards our hotel. The subway stop is a few blocks from our hotel, so these newfound cousins of mine walk us the entire way back. We all hugged and said, "We'll be seeing you." It was so nice to meet you." The former of those two statements rang quite true for me. It was a pleasure meeting this couple that I now consider part of my clan. I genuinely enjoyed sharing a meal with them. Then returning from our destination in a very scrunched, busy, unfamiliar subway ride. I always thought that New Yorkers had this pompousness about them that made them hold their head a little higher simply due to their geographical location. This trip has taught me not to judge on presumed ideas planted by other people but instead to experience things for myself before coming to any conclusions. As this sweet couple that I now call my cousins could have just as easily been living in Sioux Falls. They were such real, authentic people. Neither one of them frequented a barber shop or hair stylist, as they cut each other's hair to save money. "How cool.", I thought. I am a part of such a big family spanning across our great nation. Knowing that I have this pea-sized being in my womb, who will soon be joining this Walter tribe, made my heart swell. I felt like a part of something so much bigger than myself. "Plunk. Thud." A couple more bricks fall from my heart's wall as Betty and I walk back to our hotel room for the last time.

I love being a pregnant, stay-at-home mom. Especially during these Spring months, while the weather is still cool enough to go on our daily adventures. I knew I had a purpose. God is using me to knit a body for the soul that had already taken residence in my womb. All the while, I cared for our freshly turned four-year-old princess. I was truly a mama bear. I was leery of any man that became close to her or asked to hold her. I was ready to go for the jugular if any man looked at my precious girl with deception in his eyes. Thankfully, my exposed claws never had to pierce the flesh of any man. That mama bear in me continues to patrol the invisible bubble of observation that I have placed around Savannah. This new life of mine has me blocked in with its encircling sanity. This feels uncomfortable for me. Sometimes it is hard for me to process how normal everybody is. I can feel it again. My brain's neurons are circuiting out. Too much normalcy. It's all too immense for this fractured brain to comprehend.

On the second visit to my obstetrics doctor, it was time for my four-month ultrasound. Tim and I have previously decided to find out the gender of our second child. We had to find out. Savannah would talk to her baby sister through my tummy and tell her of all the fun they would have together once she was born. We tried to reason with this four-year-old drama queen, telling her that there is a good possibility that the baby may be a boy. "But baby girl, you know that you may be talking to your brother." I would plead with her as I pointed to my now apparent baby bump. "Nope." she would state with absolute certainty. As she would shake her tiara-topped head, with her arms crossed firmly in front of her and her bottom lip puckered up and out. Her body language silently affirms her reality that we are most definitely having a baby girl. Because of this, we were ready to discover the sex of this baby. In order that we might brace for the complete breakdown of our little drama queen if she had indeed been talking to her little brother through my belly this entire time, Tim and Savannah sit together in the cramped ultrasound room as my doctor says, "Yep. There it is. You are most assuredly having a baby boy!" My ears were waiting for the screams and cries because of the false reality she had formed for herself. But Savannah gave no response. Standing quietly, with her sun hat atop her princess head and her dollie tucked haphazardly under her arm. Observing her lack of reaction, I am sure she is not understanding what the doctor has just told us. I turn my head towards her, inquiring, "Do you understand that, Savannah? You are having a baby brother, not a baby sister." With an upturned lip, she shrugs her shoulders and gives her Dollie a big hug in the excitement of it all. Well, my daughter just surprised the hell out of me. She is our first-born. We dote over her, boast to everyone about her, and definitely over-protect her. She is our princess and our drama queen, and she has certainly never stepped out of that character she was born (or is it mostly shaped) into. Yet here, in this ultrasound room, she steps off her stage and immediately accepts the fact that the baby growing within my belly is her baby brother, not the baby sister that she was so certain of. As I confirm the facts with her, she gives her dollie a tight squeeze. I was expecting hysterical cries and tantrums that could not be calmed. However, she loves without borders. How amazing is the unconditional love of a four-year-old?

Throughout that summer, Savannah and I go on an extra amount of adventures together so that I can have this precious one on one time with her before her sibling is born. We go to Falls Park and wade through the shallow lake waters the river has created with its overflow. We are in search of anything natural. We see frogs leaping and birds swooping and diving in the river in hopes of finding lunch. We pick up small, pretty pebbles and put them in our wet, dirty pockets. We see a school of tiny fish that scatter as Savannah tries to scoop one out of the water. We would go to the zoo and have picnic lunches. Real ones. The kind where you sit on a checkered blanket and have a basket filled with summer's fresh fruit, along with other interesting edibles. Savannah and I sucked the marrow out of that summer, enjoying everything it had to offer.

As the summer is winding down, my belly is not. We only had a few months left before this baby boy would be born, and we did not have room for him at our home. Tim continues to be our sole breadwinner. We already have our current house paid off, which is such a blessing for this growing family of ours. After searching countless hours for our new home, we ended up buying one quite a reach from our target price range, but it had all the features we were looking for in a newly upgraded home. Most importantly, it had three nice-sized bedrooms, all on one level. Like finding a pearl in the ocean. As we walked through the home for the second time, we knew this was it, our new forever home. The sellers and we decided on a price and a closing date. July of next year, contingent on selling our current house, which was a starter home and a quick sell.

The next few months pass by pleasantly uneventfully. However, I do experience a lot of flaming heartburn throughout my third trimester. So many people tell me that it means my baby will be born with a full head of hair. What would we do without old wives' tales to keep us informed? Thank goodness for the progression of technology that has brought us the internet for today's new moms and dads. Much more reliable information at your fingertips.

I brought up the prospective baby name that had been rolling around in my head. "Isaac Jacob Walter," I proposed to Tim. He liked the name for good reason. Jacob was his grandpa's name, and Isaac was his great-grandpa's name. I was unaware of this while choosing it. We thought it was too big to be a coincidence. I knew this was the name destined for this baby boy. Isaac was perfectly content within the walls of my warm, comforting womb. So content that he stayed there two weeks too long. Our OB doctor explained to us how it can be unhealthy to let the pregnancy go past fourteen days overdue. She scheduled the labor induction for early the next morning. Thinking about having my labor induced with an IV Pitocin drip made me apprehensive. I have heard horror stories from my other moms that have had to go through it. Although no fear could overcome the intense expectation of meeting my son tomorrow. Despite the fact that I am completely exhausted, sleep escapes my grasp as my mind ponders tomorrow's arrival. I want my delivery to be natural. No drugs and no epidurals, all me. Laying in bed, I go through my list of things to bring: my peaceful Bohemian Monk's musical CD, tennis balls for back pressure massaging, an ice pack for my forehead, lavender scents, chapstick, and several other comfort items that I read about in one of my many books. My mind began to wander, and my extensive thoughts took a pause, allowing me to sleep for a bit. "What the...?!?" An intense abdominal cramp awakens me. Being in that freshly awoken stupor, I brush it off as heavy heartburn and try to go back to sleep. Just drifting off to dreamland and "Pang!" My abdomen was experiencing some offsetting distress as this long contraction refuses to let me sleep. My tiredness leaves me and is replaced by pure exhilaration. I am in labor! Instead of being induced in the morning, my husband grabs our go bag, and we speed to the ER. I was immediately moved to my labor suite in the OB ward of our large local hospital. Once checked in and all hooked up to the monitors, my labor pains increase to a most intolerable level and my rest periods become shorter as each painful contraction lengthens. I am finding it hard to endure the nearly constant pain. The nurse comes into my room to monitor my laborious progress. "Still a four." She announces to the entire room as she snaps her gloves off and flings them in the trash. "But I was at four when I came in this morning," I complain to whoever will listen to my laborious woes. I was in such agony. My extreme cramping hurt so bad, and so often, I was sure that I would pass out from its intense sensation ripping through my abdomen. The nurse once again offered me the epidural and I relent, allowing her to call the anesthesiologist. I cry. Not out of happiness, knowing that pain relief is on its way, but because, once again, I feel like a failure. Instead of being able to say, "I had him naturally." I have become the mom that couldn't take it. That simply gave up and settled for the relief offered to me when the pain got too tough. "Loser." I reminded myself who I am. Even through the searing pain, I am not progressing at all, and the peaceful CD playing in the background is starting to drive me crazy, and I'd like to throw those tennis balls out the window. I do not want anyone to touch me, let alone have some sort of massage. My well laid out labor pain relief plans have failed me. My mind is yelling at me, "You wimp! Do you know how many moms have gone through this before you? Why couldn't you stick to the plan? Why do you have to be such a baby all the time?" The nurse cut off my barrage of self-insults when she entered my room, accompanied by the anesthesiologist. Once the epidural is inserted, with some difficulty, my entire body goes numb from mid-chest all the way down to my toes. Couldn't feel anything. Instead of writhing in pain, I was sitting up in my bed, talking with the many guests in my room, eagerly anticipating Isaac's birth. My mom and two sisters, along with their two daughters and my husband, are all in my room in deep anticipation of the inevitable birth of this baby boy. Tim's mom periodically peeks in to see how things are going. Dressed in hospital scrubs in the middle of her shift, she says she'll stop back around her dinner break to check on us. The boys, including my brother-in-law, nephews and other close friends, were waiting in the extensive lobby area. They had no problem steering clear until they get the good word that Isaac has been born and everything unmentionable is out of sight. Boys!

"Okay, I think you are ready, missy. You are at 10 centimeters. Let me go call your doctor.", the nurse reported with relief and encouragement. Because of the overdose of epidural medication, I have no sensation past my mid-chest line. Due to this temporary numbing paralysis, I have absolutely no urge to push. I feel nothing. My nurse would carefully watch the screen that has been monitoring my contractions. Once the line reached its peak, she would bolster out, "Push!" I gave it my everything. I figured that I would have to strain that much more since I cannot feel that natural urge to push. After I have given it my all, I fall back into the bed to rest until my next upcoming push. But then I hear life's most beautiful sound. My baby's first cry. Because of my extraordinary effort, Isaac's head is out with my first big push. "Okay, Liz. Take a break." I hear my doctor instruct me as she clears the mucous from our baby's nose and mouth. "Oh, no! Did I push too hard, hurting my baby Isaac? What is going on?" My thoughts go wild as my concern escalates. My doctor comes up from her position to tell me that my bladder has become too full to push again. I haven't urinated since my epidural was inserted several hours earlier. Without any abdominal sensation, I didn't even think about it. So my doctor decided to catheterize me. She felt we ran a risk of my entire bladder bursting if we were to carry on. Thank the good Lord that I had a conscientious doctor who observed the entire situation and immediately assessed and acted conservatively to avoid an emergency of catastrophic proportions. As she advanced the tubing into my overfilled bladder, directly above Isaac's freshly pushed-out head, I watched as my husband turned green right before my eyes. My sister told him to go sit down, and he obliged her without any hesitation. "Okay, Liz. Let's try this again." My nurse instructs me as she closely watches my monitor screening my contractions. By this time, Tim is back up and by my bedside. His mom, just checking in, passed the privacy curtain, enabling her to witness the miraculous birth of her grandson. "Now, push." The nurse states with urgency and authority. Isaac is officially born at 3:45 pm, November 28th, 2000. Everyone in my hospital room, including the staff, cheered with jubilee at his birth. The doctor lays him on my chest, and I am overcome by how perfect he is, and tears stream down my face. He tries to open his eyes, but his sensitivity to the bright lights are overwhelming, and he abruptly shuts them tightly. The nurse briefly takes him to the warming station, already within my room, so that they can perform routine newborn medical necessities. He received a shot, got some goop in his eyes, and they weighed him. As the nurses continued their assessment of newborn baby Isaac, I could see his proud daddy cooing over him, as Tim's smile was from ear to ear. The nurses handed him back to me so that I could nurse him for the first time. Once that baby-sized tummy was comfortably full, we invited virtually the entire lobby inside our room. Thank goodness for the birthing suite that accommodated our large group.

There were over twenty people in my hospital room that day, all celebrating the birth of Isaac. I soaked it all in. Love filled the air with a light, refreshing mist. These were my people, here to see and hold the newest member of our tribe. "Thud, thud, plunk." I can feel them tumble down to the gigantic heap of discarded bricks laying outside a mid-sized wall encircling my heart. I glance down at my sweet baby boy wrapped snugly in his receiving blanket, asleep in his momma's arms.

Savannah, being the big sister, was promised that she could hold her baby brother first before anyone else in our enormous extended family. I can remember how she sat up so tall as she gently wrapped him up in her precious four-year-old arms. She was truly captivated by this new baby brother of hers. With her pudgy, little hands, she lightly touched each one of his tiny, wrinkled fingers and held his precious hands. She appeared to be mesmerized by this miniature-sized human she was holding onto. I feel so complete. I lovingly observe their interaction from my hospital bed. My baby girl, holding her newborn baby brother, with Tim sitting closely beside them. What an undeniably, amazing family we are. These people are my home. I possess some of the sweetest pictures from that day. Both tangible and mental. Memories never to be forgotten.

Living in our quaint, nostalgic first home was extremely snug for several months before we were able to move. Isaac's bassinet stayed in our bedroom, although he slept with us every night. This is the second child that I was raising. "Screw the books. I'm trusting my gut instincts this go around." As winter snows collect outside our picture stained-glass window, Savannah, Isaac, and I are safe and warm in the home, Tim supplied for us through his sweat and hard work. I am so grateful for my husband. Although I do not show it near enough. He is a born provider. Being a former Marine, Tim saw life in black and white. There were no exceptions. No gray areas existed in his mind. He was clean and orderly, always reliable, taking every responsibility with absolute seriousness and devotion. He is loyal to a fault. A definite family man through and through. Despite his never-ending love and his above-and-beyond husband qualities, I continued to hold back. My past was clinging to me, beckoning my many insecurities. My brain could not discriminate between normalcy and what the events of my past had taught me. The people, the relentless fear and uncontrollable fright. The events of times past remain as close to me as my very breath itself. "Do not trust anyone and tell no one." This has become my mantra through every bit of this life of mine. My paranoia would hold me captive with its wild concoctions. I was always waiting for the wrecking ball to drop, smashing me into a million pieces. I feel more than fractured. I am broken.

Thus far, I've been able to keep up this perfect mom and perfect wife facade. "Nobody is any the wiser." My mind would reassure me that my crazy isn't showing through. How could anyone know that I am an actress on a stage and, to date, I have dutifully remained in character. As a result of this portrayal, I have always envied my husband. Tim's character isn't a character at all. It is hard for me to comprehend his genuineness. It is such a rare quality.

As the winter breezes blow their last and the spring flowers begin to bloom, the kids and I are off on our outside adventures. Having a five year old and a baby, the outdoors becomes a wonderland for all to play within, and at the same time, a necessary sanctuary for me. I didn't think I could play one more game of Candyland. Savannah doesn't allow cheating, so the game could go on for hours. She was a straight arrow, just like her daddy. Later that spring, we purchased a zoo membership and would visit the animals often. City parks were a favorite too. Anywhere to explore. Isaac, my "wash and wear" kiddo, would enjoy our outdoor adventures. He appreciated the fresh air. We would go anywhere to gain access to some elbow room. Our sweet, older home is getting smaller day by day. We eagerly await the day we turn our calendars from June to July, the closing date of our spacious, new forever home.

# Chapter 6

# The Monster Inside

As we rush home from the title company this first day of July, we are overwhelmed by an endless number of family and friends already there at the cute little house that we have outgrown. We filled two full-size moving trucks and numerous pick-up loads. No one could imagine how I packed all that stuff in that tiny house. Our new house was nearly double in size and it fits us just fine. It took all of us the entire light of day to move every piece of furniture and each last box into our new forever home. "Pizza, Anyone?" We had every chair, stool and overturned bucket we owned placed in our new, box-filled dining room. As we all sat for a well-deserved rest, we filled our bellies with Papa John's Pizza and Coca-Cola. Looking around the dining room at all the people with bruised shins and smiling faces, I feel true gratitude. We are blessed to have all these people in our moving crew today. Members of our tribe, right alongside us all day, trudging up and down the stairs. With muscles, as well as patience, flexed to their maximum capacities. Now our work is done. As I finished my pizza, I found that it wasn't the food that filled me but rather the fellowship. I could hear my family and friends gut-busting laughter fill our new home with its joyful noise and its light, airy feeling. To be present. What a gift it is.

Waking up the first morning in our new home felt surreal.

Isaac, my current alarm clock that, coincidentally has no snooze button, awakens me much too early. He and I sit in our new living room with our oversized chocolate lab laying close beside me. Silence could not be found within our resonating joy. Isaac loved all the room there was to crawl around, and he appreciated the new avenues he had to explore.

A couple of hours later, Tim and Savannah slowly awaken and make their way down the long hallway to our living room. Isaac and I are already deep into a children's book. They greeted us with the same smiles that Isaac and I awoke with. The smile hints at amazement. Amazed at the house we've made our home. Our kitchen seems gigantic in the process of making our first meal together. Delicious breakfast of pancakes, eggs and bacon. A Walter favorite.

The rest of the summer passed by in a whirlwind as we stayed active and constantly on the move. I kept busy unpacking when time allowed for it, and we continued to go on daily adventures when Tim was at work. Every day held a different excursion for my two little ones and me. Swinging Savannah in the park while brother Isaac looks on from the safety of his stroller. Fishing in the perpetually stocked pond at The Outdoor Campus while the sun reflected off the water like little sparkles scattered on the surface of the pond. To beat the summer heat, we would adventure to The Old Courthouse Museum for story time with a playfully fun craft that matched the theme from the story. Another regular activity was a trip to our public library every week. We would sit on their kid-themed carpeting, reading books about zebras, tigers, and bears, which brings me to our next adventure, The Great Plains Zoo. We sat on the bench directly outside the monkeys' cage as they put on a show for us. Anytime, as long as they could sense our presence, they would gracefully swing from branch to branch. One monkey skillfully somersaults through the air. His outstretched hand confidently reaches for the rope that he seems to grab hold of just in the nick of time. I enjoyed seeing those precious smiles on both of my children's faces. I loved them so much. Once our daily adventure would come to an end, we would buckle up and drive home in our new, dark green minivan.

By mid-August, we had the house arranged and even had a garage sale to clear all the unnecessary clutter and make some extra cash while we were at it. During nap time, I would clean like a mad woman, picking every toy off the floor, clearing every dish and wiping down every surface. I wanted my husband to come home to a freshly cleaned house. Which he seldom did. Each day after their naps were over, my two little tikes would need a snack and then proceed to play with each toy as they lay strewn across the living room floor. Every surface had tiny fingerprints of dirt and food covering it. Looking back now, I wonder why I wasted all that precious time. I was trying so hard to be the ideal wife and the most perfect mom. I kept an exceptionally clean house while still managing to have happy kids that I endlessly entertained, no matter the season. The blistering hot sun, or a bitter, cold, snowy day, I could find an activity that would bring joy to my little ones. My husband perpetually gives me a kiss before leaving for work and upon his return home, I could expect a peck on the cheek from him. We were living in our virtual dream home. Everything was so perfect. I had successfully pulled the wool over everyone's eyes. I remained in character. Stoic with my emotions. Fighting the demons from my past that constantly pulled at me. I would stand in our front yard, playing with my kiddos, as I have endless small talk with my preppy neighbors. I was keeping it all together. I exemplified the perfect stay-at-home mom and wife. I was living out my pretend white picket fence life until I wasn't…

My family's entire world was rocked by an extreme earthquake that I was responsible for. The plates shifted deep within my soul, creating enormous tremors that would upset our entire world. My fractured brain couldn't keep up the charade any longer. I was so good at hiding all of my infinite secrets, stored away in a heavily bolted vault. I always held my true self back and out of sight while playing my part perfectly. I'm not sure why because the show was not over, yet I stepped out of character. That likable, normal character that I created had taken stage left as she slipped behind the curtain and out of sight.

# FACING IT

This is where my story turns to sadness and depression. It becomes graphic and chaotic and so very far from perfect.

Sometime after Savannah started kindergarten that August, my thoughts began to fiercely encourage me to hurt myself. At the beginning of that autumn season, I gave in to my constant urges and made my first cut. I was a beautiful young mom and wife. Yet, for some reason, when naptime came for little Isaac, I gently closed his door and locked myself in the bathroom. I lay out my special tools on a tissue placed on the bathroom counter. Those tools consisted of anything sharp. It began with needles of any kind. If that wasn't available, I used paper clips and a pair of small scissors from our sewing kit. Slanted or pointed tweezers were also a favorite. All my caustic instruments were laid out on the clean, white tissue, resembling surgical tool placement. I turned the bathroom door knob to ensure it was locked. Out of absolute randomness, I hastily grab ahold of one of my penetrating implements. This first episode, I chose the long, thick needle. Once I had it penetrated through the skin of my chin, I threaded it through the flesh beneath until the heavy bore needle poked out the other side, creating a deep one-inch stitch. I affix the needle so that it is sticking out equally on both sides. Taking a deep inhalation, my fingers take hold of each end of that needle threaded deep within my chin and pull with full force, ripping through the flesh underneath my tool's thick steel bore.

Blood and bits of tissue splatter on the mirror as a river of deep red blood poured from the gaping wound I have just constructed on my face. With my pulse quickening, I would futilely attempt to grab towels to cover the deep wound, as the blood drips its large, scarlet drops to the rug beneath my feet. As they hit the floor, they would burst into big red stains. My adrenaline has reached its fight-or-flight plateau. I looked at the time on my bloody phone to clarify how long I have been in this hellish bathroom. Time seems to stand still when I am in this state of psychosis. I put pressure on my chin while using a wet bath towel to clean the mirror and sink. I can feel each of my nerves on their end as I wonder what the hell just happened. This is the day that changed my very identity. That moment in time lit something inside of me. Something that nobody would want. My perfectly scripted character and the fake facade that had become my life all came crashing down before me. This slice of my existence would define the rest of my life. I frantically try to fill the newly clotted, gaping wound with liquid makeup and way too much loose powder. I had to continually return to our bathroom, refilling the powder to fill the emptiness that now resided in my flesh.

Isaac awoke from his nap just as I finished cleaning up the bathroom. Once I stepped across the threshold of his room, I put on my happy face and tried to return to the perfect mother I was before his nap. But everything had changed. I have changed.

Once it was five o'clock, my anxiety peaks once again,

wondering what my husband will say to me. Upon returning home from work, he couldn't help but notice the open lesion on my face, surrounded by thick makeup. I cried. The storm cloud of shame hung over my head as it rained down its spears of guilt upon me. The sheer dread I felt, unable to understand what the hell had happened to me. The degrading embarrassment of having this self-inflicted wound on my face. Sheer terror rips my body to its core. I dreaded the look as I gazed into my husband's eyes. He met me back with an expression of shock and disbelief. He questioned me incessantly.

I made up a makeshift excuse that was completely unsustainable. I didn't want him to know the truth. He married a monster. That evening, I continually checked my face in the mirror, ensuring the hole on my chin still existed. I could see my husband watching me that night. He had a look of utter disgust on his face. I understood him. I was disgusted with myself too. In the past, I knew I was playing the part. Once I stepped off my counterfeit stage, I instantly stepped onto the stage of a horror movie with me playing the lead. "What the hell is happening to me?" Unfortunately, that incredible urge to hurt myself was like a switch that my fractured brain had engaged on that fateful day.

The next morning, Savannah left on the school bus en route for her full day of kindergarten. I knew she wasn't an idiot. My daughter left for school that day knowing something drastic had just changed in her life. Tim gave me his usual goodbye kiss and told me to be good. That made me feel worse. I knew what I did was bad. It was as if I had lost control of my mind and body once I locked myself behind our bathroom door. Alone in the house with little Isaac, my gut wrenches with anticipation of what the future day would hold for me. How could I have known I was at the beginning of a twenty-year horror flick with me playing the lead role. Every day, I continued to take advantage of Isaac's nap times to satisfy my psychotic urges. All the while struggling to be that perfect mom.

Once the winter winds began to blow, Isaac and I continued to have our nearly daily excursions to the library, the museum, the Washington Art Pavilion and The Outdoor Campus. I deliriously hoped that if I kept up the repetitive actions that he was accustomed to, I could keep this new reality from his precious, innocent blue eyes. Each and every adventure we were on, people would stare at me endlessly and whisper amongst themselves, "What happened to her?" "Is it contagious?" Their whispers blared loudly in my overwrought ears. My perfect facade blown to bits right in front of me, with its shrapnel shooting past my ears and lodging deep within my heart. I felt defeated. It was so apparent to the world that something was wrong with me.

Isaac was now one year old and was running everywhere he went. He and I continued to enjoy our daily endeavors wherever they took us. When it was nearing 3 o'clock, we would pick up Savannah from kindergarten. We would walk up, past the play equipment, to the school's side door. This is where all the other parents gathered to await that last bell, signaling the end of another school day. All of the children rush out of the double doors and greet their parents. I held my face low, my eyes pointed towards the ground, trying to avert the stares of the other parents. On the drive home, I would talk myself into the amnesia of this new erratic person I had become so that I could still be that forfeited perfect mom for my precious babies.

I continued performing all the normal activities I did as the perfect mom. I played with my children incessantly and was there for all their needs. I had dinner warm and ready when my husband returned home from work. I was loyal, responsible, hard-working, and reliable. It wasn't what I did that mattered, though. It is who I was.

I continued hurting the same area on my chin until that initial cut now involved my entire chin, with a deep serrated lesion that nearly cut my chin in two horizontally. One day, my husband came home unexpectedly when I was in the middle of my debasing project behind the locked door of the bathroom. The room was covered with my bright red blood. It splattered the mirror, filled the sink and sprinkled the floor with its large scarlet drops. It probably goes without saying that he was in utter shock. He made me show him. I moved the blood-soaked gauze I was using to apply pressure to the deep lesion encompassing my chin. Once he saw the enormous chasm, he gasped, opening his mouth wide open in utter terror. He began to frantically clean up my blood as if he were hiding a murderous scene. I left the room, sobbing. I realized this sweet boy in the dark flannel shirt was scared of me and frightened of what I've become. I felt unlovable. I was too fractured. I couldn't understand me, so how the hell was he supposed to? His lack of attention toward me made me feel worse. I knew this was all too much for him to take. I tried to protect him from me from the start. Buried deep within my soul, I knew that a monster had resided. I didn't expect that inner monster to attack my face with such a vengeance. The sum of my past, the heavy feeling of guilt from events that I feel I should have prevented, the constant fear of never knowing what disaster would strike next, the shame of each and every wickedness I allowed to happen. That little girl inside me has exposed herself as my worst enemy. Fear and anxiety pumped through my arteries as guilt and shame returned through my veins. Such agony enveloped me that I could physically feel this heavy sensation in my heart, as it would increase several beats with each mounting compulsion to hurt myself. The plastic mannequin I had formed over my true self had given way, like a dam crumbling under the pressure of the overflowing waters within its banks.

After that episode, Tim prompted me to make a doctor's appointment. I didn't feel human when I sat in the waiting room of the dermatologist's office, with two extra large bandages covering my chin. Everyone else in the waiting room looked pretty normal and routine. I, on the other hand, couldn't even sit still. My legs were bouncing up and down in nervous anticipation of my appointment. Nobody but Tim has seen how far I have taken it. I was not looking forward to removing my bandage for the doctor and then sheepishly explaining how it happened. "Elizabeth Walter", the nurse called my name to come back. My gut wrenched, and my mind desperately searched for a soft opening to my story of pure psychosis. I also dread the looks on people's faces when they see what I have done to myself. The doctor decided to concentrate on healing my chin, to avoid surgical measures. It was an ebb and flow of good days and bad, but eventually, several months later, my chin was healed.

My face was back intact. My chin was heavily scarred, but at least it was healed. I was so grateful to my doctor. Because of this, I felt human again. Fractured but lovable. I felt like an acceptable member of society once again, instead of the outcast I had been.

Our lives never returned to normal, albeit this did feel much better. I didn't have to hide my face or avert my eyes. People would comment on my scar tissue often. "What happened to your chin?" This became the usual question I would be asked by mere strangers in the grocery store. People can be so stupid at times. "Let me tell you my life story as we pick through these roma tomatoes." Idiots. My normal response was silence. But their questions had an effect on my spirit. I would begin to question myself and remember all those times locked up with my psychosis behind the bathroom door. That monster within me felt alive and well. My mind fought the impulses that resided within me daily as Isaac, and I drove home from the grocery store.

Around this same time, my husband and I discussed changing churches and denominations. St Michael's was on the other side of town, making it over an hour of driving time round trip. He had been listening to Christian radio and decided to try an open bible church only three blocks away from our house. Rustic Hills Community Church consists of approximately one hundred families, which is a small-sized church for Sioux Falls. Upon arriving, we are immediately greeted by the pastor's wife, who isn't shy about giving hugs and welcoming us to the church. I fell in love with the sermons. They were so much different than the short homilies I had become accustomed to at the Catholic church. They withheld much more information. Nearly every parishioner brought their bibles with them and would look up scripture right along with the pastor during the message. During one of those sermons, Pastor Mike encouraged us to read our bible. He continued to mention it in nearly every sermon for a while and made up special pamphlets on how to read the bible in one year. I took this challenge on with fire in my soul. I have always loved God's word. I know He has always been with me. Even before I knew who He truly was, He was there. We all knew we had found our new church home.

Of course, being in scripture daily increased my spirituality and the level of intimacy I had with my Lord. I easily read through the bible in a year with true joy in my heart. I felt close to the Lord. I decided to read the bible again the following year, with a different version for some variety. During Sunday morning sermons, I would soak up all the knowledge like a sponge. I would constantly take notes so that I could review it all later. I felt alive with God's Word buried deep within my heart. I prayed earnestly for Him to take this psychotic portion of my brain away from m me.

Isaac began kindergarten in 2006, which left me home alone for the day until it was time to pick up Savannah. By the time we returned home, Isaac would be arriving about thirty minutes later via school bus.

It felt much different being home alone after I had been kept busy with my kiddos for nearly ten years. This is when my psychosis became worse. Tim was the last one to leave the house at 8 o'clock for work, giving me several hours alone.

Throughout the previous years, I have continued to injure my face, but to a lesser degree. I would follow the same pattern and use the same sharp tools but would make more superficial cuts. Lesions that would form an eschar and be healed within three weeks or so. After having the entire house to myself for a few days, my psychotic brain relentlessly prompted me to hurt myself. When this overwhelming compulsion embodies me, my pulse quickens to a rapid beat, and my respirations increase almost to the point of hyperventilation. My hands tremble. These impulses of mine are so strong they resemble instinctual behavior. One day, I relented. I had just returned home from dropping off Savannah at school, so I knew I had ample time. I found my tools hidden beneath my headbands where I had last left them. I lay them out on a clean, white tissue. My hand finds the sharp, pointed scissors. As I poke the point of my instrument into my heavily scarred skin, I felt resistance. The scar tissue had become so tough I had to use an extra amount of strength to poke the scissors through its tough exterior. Once through, the blood begins to drip from my chin. I hold my face over the bathroom sink in hopes of catching all the scarlet drops. I then proceeded to dig those scissors into the scar tissue beneath, leaving a good two-inch cut. As my skin continues to bleed a scarlet stream into the sink, I moved the bloody, pointed scissors to the left side of my nose and dug in with the same force I had used on my chin. This left a gaping hole in the side of my nose that burrowed its way all the way through to the inside of my nostril. I finally stopped out of pure exhaustion. I now notice how blood has covered the bathroom. The floor was sprinkled with its large droplets, and the sink had a film of thick blood encircling it. The mirror was splattered with my blood and flecks of tissue. I looked at my blood-soaked phone to see the time. I had to take a second glance, as I couldn't believe my eyes. It was time to leave to pick up Savannah. I had been in that bathroom all day. I hurriedly cleaned up the best I could and left to get to Savannah.

Upon arriving home for work, Tim looked at me with the same disgrace I had become accustomed to. It hurt me so much. I wanted him to give me his strength and pull me out of the abyss that had become my life. Instead, I only felt judged. Not just by him, or strangers, or the rest of my family, but loathed by me. I hated myself to the very core of my being. I cursed the day I was born and wished it could be erased from history.

A couple of weeks later, I noticed some odd-looking drainage from the hole that burrowed through my nose, so I hesitantly went to the ER. They immediately admitted me and started an IV drip, administering a strong antibiotic for my infected wounds. I was in the hospital for several days. Upon returning home, I was glad to have received the medicines I needed but was leary of entering the devil's lair once again. Over the time span of several months, the side of my nose and chin were healed. But this was just the beginning.

Tim continued to work as a locksmith during the day and took on a second job in the evenings. He employed himself as a hawk, hovering over me, watching my every move. If I went into the bathroom, he would stand right outside the door and wait. If I occupied it for a second longer than two minutes, he would pound on the door, like the SWAT team wanting to gain entrance. This only served to increase my anxiety, but it was how he was dealing with it, I guess.

I was enjoying a few months with a healed face, for the most part. Like I said before, my psychotic tendencies never left me. For some reason, after a total catastrophe of my making, I would slow down on the depths of my injuries, making more superficial wounds with my scathing hidden tools. But it never stopped. My mind was depressed when I wore large self-inflicted wounds on my face, and it constantly fights the demons whispering atrocities in my tender, vulnerable ears.

I made an appointment at the Mayo Clinic. It is there that I was diagnosed with PTSD. The psychiatrist told me he thought that is why I continued to hurt myself. I have had night terrors ever since this debasing disorder started. Sleep escaped me as my demons went to bed with me. They would shred all my dreams, and I bled on my sheets. "Why is this my life?"

One evening, while on vacation visiting my brother and his wife in Michigan, I took the entire bottle of my anti-anxiety medications in hopes of not waking up in the morning. I'd also had a few beers with dinner, so I was comfortably numb. Right before drifting off, I told my husband what I had done. He sat beside me all night as I slept. Waking up the next morning was a downer for me. Tim told me that I went through several episodes of apnea, lasting nearly a minute each time. Just as his fright increased, I gasped and returned to breathing normally. He disclosed this to me after our breakfast together. I got close, but I missed my target, and so my life goes on.

Once Autumn was upon us and the kids had returned to school, I had all day to myself in the peak of my psychosis. On an ordinary day, I carefully lay my sharp items on their white, clean tissue on the plain bathroom counter. I am calm as I prepare myself for battle. A battle in which there is one lone soldier and no winners. I preemptively grab one tissue after another until I have a large handful. These are to catch the blood I know is soon coming. As my urge intensifies, I can feel my heart pounding within my chest wall, quickening its pulse with each beat. My breaths are shallow and resemble the panting of a tired dog after a long walk in the hot sun. My skin feels numb all over. It is hard to explain the unfathomable, unrelenting, feverish urge. The entirety of myself needed to hurt and injure my face. I passionately desired to cut it, rip it and pull at it until it broke open into a wound that became worse with each one of my bad episodes. My hand is deliberate as I slip the pointed side of my slanted tweezers deep into my cheek. Cutting through my flesh until I can feel the tip of the tweezers touch my gums. I have rigorously cut through the flesh of my cheek. It is about a two-inch laceration that showed my teeth through its opening. Once I see my efforts in the mirror, my heart sinks into my gut. "What have I done now?" I knew that no amount of medicine or visits to the dermatologist could fix what I have just chiseled into my once pretty face.

I waited several weeks to seek medical assistance. Every day, several times a day, I would heavily rebandage my vacant flesh as the wound seeped massively. Day by day, I observed the gigantic dissection growing more hideous as the freshly cut flesh began to pucker, making the wound appear even larger. At last, several weeks later, the fear of losing my entire face overcame the fear I had of seeking medical attention. My fingers glanced at the plastic surgeons listed in the yellow pages. I decided on a female. Dr. Karu. I explained my situation, and the receptionist scheduled me an emergency appointment for the following day. As I waited for my name to be called, my anxiety had reached its peak.

I longed to jump out of my own skin. "Elizabeth," the nurse calls me back. Dr. Karu was gentle with me. I did not feel the same amount of shame I had with doctors in the past. She measured and photographed my unbelievable wound, sculpted by my own hand. After her full assessment, she scheduled surgery for the following day. I was nervous with anticipation. She was going to fix what I had broken. Once the medical staff had moved me onto the hard, cold surgery table, fear took hold of me. My anesthesiologist placed the mask over my face and told me to count back from ten. Without even realizing any time had passed, I was in the recovery room. I experienced extreme pain surrounding my cheek. The surgical area was covered with a heavy bandage that I was instructed to keep on until my follow-up appointment in a week. Seven days after my surgery, she removed my dressing. I held back my tears in her office as I silently choked with dread at the deep indentation left on my face. It made me realize that my hurts and injuries could never be fully restored. I had become scar face. I had just completed the first of four surgeries that Dr. Karu would have to perform to complete the skin graft on my cheek.

After those bushel of plastic surgeries, I admitted myself to the third floor of our Behavioral Health Unit. It was an in-house treatment for those of us that are so broken we need to seek intense therapy to try to survive our messed up lives. I hated it. There were thick, black steel bars on all the windows. Upon being admitted, they did a full body check. This meant that I stood in a room, naked and shivering, both from the coolness of the air and my nerves being on end. All the while being inspected by several employees that would not stop staring at this crazy woman in front of them. They went through everything I had brought and took away most of it. They allowed me one pair of sweatpants and five shirts. No books, no phone or radio. Nothing that may bring pleasure. We were not allowed to have anything dangerous, which included a decent writing instrument. Short, red, blunt pencils were my only means of writing

Each and every employee acted like they were so far above all of the patients. It was like the warden with his guards at a prison. We each were required to see a psychologist every day for one hour. I told them what they wanted to hear so that I could leave this hell that I had willingly walked into. After my initial three days, I was discharged. I was so good at pretending, I had fooled them all. I left that dungeon even more broken than I had been upon admission. I didn't care, though. It felt horrific, and being there only served to intensify my unfathomable shame and guilt. Now, it has been confirmed. I am crazy.

Throughout these last several years, a cloud of depression has followed me wherever I went. I felt complete hopelessness. I knew my family would be better without me. If I wasn't injuring my face, I would be crying because of it. I didn't have the strength to put on my plastic mannequin and be that perfect mom. Because I knew deep down that having this disorder made me the worst mom for my precious babies.

During these times, I would cry out to my God, pleading with Him to fix this fractured brain of mine. I didn't want to be who I was. I spent an entire summer just sitting on our stoop in the garage, hidden from the world. All those moments spent sobbing over a situation that I felt unable to change. But I knew the power of my God. He spoke the word, and light appeared. He invented light with a word. I was confident in His authority. I would scream to him in agony, "I know how powerful You are, Lord. Please heal me of my affliction. I long for you to use me to be about Your work. But in my current condition, I am unable to do anything. I feel useless because I am useless. Please, Lord. Please heal me. Through Christ, my Lord and Savior, Amen."

Unfortunately, my healing did not happen like I had hoped. I soon had severed my face once again so that my lower lip and chin were virtually disconnected from each other. My lip hung loose, and my chin puckered beneath it. It was difficult to eat or drink anything in this condition. The food and liquids would spill out the perimeter of the large cut I had made. My entire face swelled up, and I resembled the elephant man. Once again, my fear and I drove to the ER. Dr. Karu immediately admitted me to the hospital for emergency antibiotics because the infection had moved to my blood. I was told later that I had almost died, and it did feel like I was laying on my deathbed. I lay comatose for one full day and in and out the next. By the third day, the antibiotics had begun killing off the bacteria that ran rampant in my system, and I was able to sit up and even talk for a spell. My facial swelling began to diminish by the fourth day. Dr. Karu would visit me often to see how things were progressing. She performed plastic surgery to repair the laceration a couple of weeks after being discharged from the hospital. My surgery went as planned, and Dr. Karu affixed my lip back up to my chin with hundreds of stitches holding it all together. I had suffered nerve damage, and the opening of my mouth had become considerably smaller. Pediatric in size. Because of these two byproducts, I experience problems eating. I can only use extra small spoons and take tiny bites. A lot of the food spills out of my mouth and onto my clothing. I can no longer sip hot coffee from the cup or gulp water when I am thirsty. I require the use of a drinking straw. Even with that implement, I have to push the straw up against the roof of my mouth with my tongue, allowing me to suck in. I have no ability to pucker my lips, making it impossible to give a goodbye kiss. The nerves and muscles have been severed in the attack upon myself. But I survived, and life went on.

I had two other grafting surgeries to repair another self-inflicted injury which left a giant open space between my lip and nose. I feel like I have visited this subject enough. I had all the same emotions, urges and feelings of my previous episodes. Just another scar to add to the face I am sculpting.

Once Isaac finished grade school, I decided to go back to work as a nurse. The scars on my face have blurred some, and I wanted to feel productive. I absolutely loved working. Helping people and supplying for their daily needs is right up my alley. My passion, really.

# FACING IT

I was so happy to be financially contributing to my family while helping those in great need. I felt fulfilled. I kept my extreme urges at bay, knowing I would have to show my face to the world the following day. I continued to make more superficial cuts that would scab over and heal within a few weeks. I made up stories to my fellow employees and the clients I serviced with the intention of hiding my underlying condition. I would tell one person it was severe psoriasis. Inform another that it was eczema. Anything to hide the truth that stood right in front of them. This seemed to work for me for a while. Tim was overjoyed that my disorder had taken a hiatus.

After a particularly hard, long day at work, I came home to an empty house. I was eager in anticipation of fulfilling this urge welling up inside my bones. My pulse quickened as I grabbed my sharp tools from their hiding place. I proceeded to cut around my upper lip in such a way that it completely dislodged from its natural position attached to the skin beside it. As I made that last cut, my lip broke free from my face on the right side. It hung loose, completely unattached to the flesh beside it. My heart sank. "Why did I do this again?"

Dr. Karu was able to fix it easier than the other cuts she had surgically repaired in the past. Because I was now employed, I immediately made an appointment instead of putting it off as I had in the past. She was able to schedule my surgery for the following week. Going to work with a bandaid covering my lip, I told the people I worked for that I had some biopsies taken. More lies. I've told so many I'm beginning to believe them myself. The surgery went well, and my lip looked way better than I thought it would. No deep indentation, no thick scar. The only clue that my surgery existed were the outside stitches lining the right side of my lip. I felt empowered returning to work, knowing that I had fooled everyone.

I continued working, but once I had satisfied that initial, familiar urge, the intensity of it increased within my body. I found myself locked within our bathroom on several occasions. I had now cut the other side of my lip, and as I made that last cut, half of my lip fell to the ground. I stared at it and muffled my screams of disbelief. I looked at my face in the mirror. I saw my reflection glaring back at me with half an upper lip intact and my front teeth and canines showing through the missing portion.

I called in sick to work and made another appointment with my plastic surgeon. She planned on scheduling my surgery for the next week until she spoke with my psychiatrist. He felt I wasn't emotionally ready for surgery. He was sure that I would continue to cut after the surgical repair. Dr. Karu had said that this would have to be my last surgery, as I did not have much healthy, unaffected skin to perform a skin flap surgery. So I continue to wear a bandage covering my absent upper lip.

# FACING IT

I quit work because I was out of excuses for my many facial injuries. I felt inept, not being able to hold down a job. I had not climbed this high, so I didn't understand how my valley could be so deep. My mind was filled with thoughts of who I truly was. Hopelessness and sadness embodies me. I managed to keep up my charade at work for seven years until that little girl inside of me came out to shake me to my very core, upsetting my entire world, again.

Being unemployed made me feel like a useless member of society. "How crazy am I that I can't even hold down a job?" My debasing thoughts filled my mind. I continue to envy Tim and his ability to remain his routine, normal self. "Why couldn't I be more like him? "Please, Dear Lord, cleanse me and make me whole again. Take away this demon that I fight against daily, pushing at the goads."

Being alone in our home all day long. A definite trigger for my self-abuse. My depression had deepened. My mind is tired of the constant self-harming thoughts and impulses, and my body is drained from carrying them out. I am hopeless.

I unlocked our safe and retrieved my husband's 9 mm Beretta from its secured case. I shoved a handful of bullets into my jean pockets and left our house for the last time. After checking into a local hotel, I quickly found my room and sat down on the edge of the bed facing the mirror. My phone is off, ensuring that I will not be disturbed. With the gun loaded and cocked, I raise it into my mouth. "Just pull the effing trigger! Can't you even off yourself the right way?" I stayed in that position for some time, with my mouth open wide, allowing the Beretta to rest on my tongue. I can sense the cold steel of the barrel in my mouth and decide this is it. "Do the world a favor. Pull the trigger." As I begin to press firmly with my index finger, I panic, immediately releasing the trigger and dropping the gun to the floor. I fell back on the bed and lay in the fetal position, weeping.

My depression is so dark. I feel cold in the shadow of my Lord. Abandoned, like an orphan who no one comes to take home with them. I have been wearing this band-aid covering my upper lip for a while now, and peoples' stares and comments still sting like tiny darts aimed for my heart. During this time, my oldest brother, Mike, was diagnosed with pancreatic cancer. I didn't know how to add this piece of life altering news to my ever-growing depression. I couldn't comprehend the "whys" of life. "Why have I suffered with this psychosis for so many years now? Why does my brother have end-stage cancer? Why?" My circuits were shorting out in my brain, making me have ugly thoughts.

I had purchased some razor blades at a local store and parked at the end of their lot, where no one could see me. The sun was setting behind me, and soon a blanket of darkness covered my world, both realistically and metaphorically. I took one sharp razor blade out, nicking my finger as I removed it from its packaging. I cut on my wrists till blood filled my clothing and the interior of the van. I couldn't make the cut deep enough to perform my intentions. "What the hell, Elizabeth. You have no problem making thick excavations in your face, yet you can't make this fateful cut deep enough." So deep that I would be leaving this parking lot in a body bag. I stayed there for hours. I have several scars that I sustained on my wrists today from that night. So many scars I possess, both seen and unseen. At my third failed attempt, I crawled to the back of our minivan and fell asleep in the cool, brisk night.

I wanted to leave this world and all it held dear behind me. I was convinced that this world would be a better place without me in it. I was ready to meet my Maker. I know He sees my heart and the waves that have tossed me to and fro, as I am overcome by the waters. I did not want to live any longer. I saw nothing good within me. I had nothing left to give. My cup is dry.

Savannah had left for college, about an hour's drive away. I know she loved being away from home, living in the dorms and making good friends. She came home a couple of times a month to visit. I was happy for her. She was away from me.

Isaac was now a freshman in high school and doing well in his studies. Scholastics have always come pretty easy for him. It was nice not having to worry about his grades. He and I would often talk about anything from his day at school to my declining mental health. He seemed to understand the darkness of depression and would empathize with me. I felt bad that both of my children have had to carry this burden with them throughout their lives. The embarrassment of a mom that comes to your band recital full of scars and bandages. I'm sure they had to experience the same stares and whispers that I had to tolerate. It wasn't fair. I wanted to be their perfect mom. "How did everything get so fucked up?"

August 13th, 2018, was the most ominous day. An accumulation of my sadness, guilt, shame, self-hatred, and deep depression had overtaken me. It is so dark I am blind to my hand in front of my face. I wanted a refund on my life. Please, take it, Lord, and give me heaven in return. After everyone had left the house that day, I began to sob without end. I walked downstairs to gather the supplies I had already pretested. I grabbed the wheeled suitcase with an extendable handle and some medium-thickness rope that I had precut. After loading that in the back of my van, I returned to our house to carry off two 35-pound weights. The most important item for the project ahead of me. I felt anxious as I loaded the van, afraid that Tim could come home unexpectedly. I placed the last weight in the van and closed its sliding door. I slipped behind the steering wheel and was on my way to Lake Alvin, about a twenty-minute drive. I rolled the windows down so that I could enjoy the feeling of the sun beating down on me while a pleasant, cool breeze blew through my hair. I feel calm. There is no screwing this one up. I would finally be successful. I pull into a parking spot on the far side of the lake that is full of foliage and mostly used by fishermen. I open the side van door, laying the black suitcase on the asphalt ground. I carefully unzip it all the way around until the lid flaps open. I place one 35-pound weight inside of the luggage and then the other. I toss the rope on top and close the zipper. Taking the handle, I haphazardly maneuver the heavy, offset suitcase down the hill to the west side of the lake. I sit in the mud, the grass and the muck. I slowly lower my suitcase to the ground, removing all of its contents. I tie one 35-pound weight to my ankle, knotting the precut rope several times to ensure it will hold. I do not take pause, as my decision has been made. I readily fasten the second 35-pound weight to my other ankle in the same fashion. I stand up and walk unsteadily to the shore of the lake. I trudge along, now up to my knees, dragging the weights banded tightly to my ankles. I take a few more steps before hitting the big drop-off that I knew existed there. My body falls to the depths of the waters. I keep my eyes open as I watch the light from above disappear as I sink further into the boundless waters. I see the last little bubbles come from my mouth as my breath escapes me and my body continues its descent. Instead of my life flashing before me, my thoughts were turned to my children's future. What would their lives become without me in it? I would not be there for their graduations or their weddings. My own grandchildren would never know me. Savannah and Isaac will have to grieve for their mother while others' whispers of my suicide enter their precious ears. "What have I done?" My thoughts went dark as my heart stopped pumping life's blood through my cold, barren body.

# Chapter 7

# Love is Stronger than Death

"Whoosh!" My body sailed through the deep waters and was thrust forward several feet. I could feel pressure being applied to my backside, resembling the sensation of a tremendous hand scooping my body from its final resting place while gently placing my feet on solid ground. I looked all around, and there was no one. I knew I had just experienced the hand of the Lord save me from myself, as deep calls to deep. A mere moment ago, I was unconscious and without the breath of life in me. I am now submerged chest-deep in the lake, coughing water out of my lungs until I throw up. I slowly trudged back to the shoreline. Each step becomes more difficult and painful than the last. The well-tied rope is burning my ankle with each movement I make.

At last, I wade towards the banks of my opened tomb. As I catch my breath from the strenuous trip back from death's sure grip, my mind is bewildered at what had transpired. I slowly untied the numerous knots securing the weights to my raw, reddened ankles. Being in the water only served to make them tighter. Those knots seemed impossible. I wondered why I hadn't brought scissors. My mind quickly finds an answer. I didn't intend on coming out of those waters. I sit here in the mud and the muck, with vibrant, green foliage surrounding me, and for the first time ever, I feel happy to be alive. At that distinct point in my life, I made a covenant with the Lord, promising Him I will retire my diligent crusade to end my life and actually start living it. It took me over an hour to free my red-hot, rope-burned ankles. It felt so good to untie that last knot and finally be free. I loaded all of my supplies back into their suitcase. My current 102-pound frame stumbles up the hill, pulling my baggage behind me.

I have lost fifty pounds throughout this depression of mine. I didn't eat. Therefore, the pounds fell off of me until there was nothing left to lose. I was a skeleton with skin, and I could feel the strain of my emaciated muscles as I finally made it to the plateau of that long hill. With the last of my strength, I loaded each individual item in the van and slid behind the steering wheel, soaking the seat beneath me. I was frigid. I shook uncontrollably. I turned the heat to full blast and began driving home. On that twenty-minute commute, my mind tried to wrap itself around what had just happened. I suppose that's what a miracle handed down from on high is like, unexplainable. God knows what He is doing, and I am just along for the ride. Today, He may not have healed all my demons, but He did breathe His life into me. I felt special. The Lord cares for low-down, rotten, good-for-nothing me. I knew I was meant to be in this world for a purpose, even if I must suffer through to find it.

Driving closer to home, I began to wonder how I would explain away the fact that I was soaking wet. Thankfully, my husband was the only one home, and I was excited to tell him my miraculous story. He was watching television and didn't give me his full attention, keeping his eyes turned towards the picture box. As I spoke my last word, he replied with a "Hmph." I stripped my wet clothes from my shivering body and took a hot shower, finally allowing the river within me to fall from my tear ducts.

I awoke the next morning to find this relentless urge to harm myself still remained within me. God saved me from the waters. He did not, however, free me of my fractured brain. I fought the urges with the same amount of strength it took to trudge back to shore that day.

I continued on my life's journey, fighting off my caustic impulses daily. Some days were a total success. Others I did fairly well, only hurting my face in a superficial sense. Then came more bad days.

Isaac is now graduating from Washington High School. He has plans on continuing his education in psychology with hopes of becoming a psychiatrist. I can see how my disorder has affected each and every aspect of my babies' lives. They desperately yearn for a world where people suffering from a mental disorder will be treated with the same amount of respect, care and dignity that a heart patient would receive. Equality. They both see a great need for equality within our healthcare system. Their eyes and ears have witnessed too many doctors deal with me harshly because they couldn't understand why I couldn't just will myself to stop. I couldn't understand it either. I was living it and knew I was powerless over my strong urges to hurt myself. Savannah and Isaac were innocent victims of my situation and the experiences that unfolded before them because of it. There is no apology that fits my crime. My precious ones remain driven, though. Life's blowbacks sometimes take pause.

Savannah has just graduated from USD with a full red cap and gown. She had majored in Healthcare Administration. Witnessing how I was treated within our healthcare system lit a fire under her. She wants to change the entirety of our local hospitals and clinics. I loved seeing my baby up there on stage, being honored for her four years of hard work. It lasted only a moment, but what a sweet moment it was. It is frozen in time within my mind forever. We had a huge party for both of their achievements at our church home, Rustic Hills. The open house was bustling with people throughout the celebration. I know my kids felt honored to have so many people in attendance. It made me happy to see their accomplishments celebrated. Their virtual constant smiles were contagious.

Throughout the busyness of two graduations to plan for, I still kept in close contact with Mike. He was currently on a chemotherapy plan that gave him one or two good days a week.

Hardly seems worth all the misery that the chemo brought to his life. But, as a good little sister, I kept my thoughts to myself. He seemed to hold onto life so tightly. I'm not really sure why.

One day, Mike called me to let me know he was done with the chemotherapy and was going to let nature take its course. His doctors had given him six months at the most. Through tear-filled eyes, I choked out, "I'm so sorry, Mike. I love you." We ended the phone call soon after. There are no words that could calm the fear and discomfort my brother was experiencing. "How unjustly ironic!" I called out to my Lord. My brother has been fighting to stay alive, and you save me, who has been struggling to find six feet under. It didn't make sense. I would have traded places with my big brother at any time. I love him so much. I would have gladly taken on his sufferings. But God chose to save me, a vagabond. I didn't understand Him at all. Salty tears rolled down my cheeks once again. I didn't want to lose my brother. He was my person. He protected me when we were young. I could fill an entire book with my big brother's life and character. But that is for another time.

Mike visited Sioux Falls in mid-August of that year. He sat on the bottom stoop of my front porch, sporting three sweatshirts in the 90-degree heat because he always felt so cold. Sitting outside, reminiscing and laughing, felt gratifying for my soul. But in the midst of the joy lingered silence, in the truth of the situation. By this time, he had a jaundice skin tone and a bald head and weighed half of what he did before the dreadful diagnosis. But when he would laugh, his eyes still sparkled, and I could see that small space between his two front teeth. It made his smile that much more captivating. Oh, how I long to see that smile again. When his trip here was through, we all stood with him at the airport, waiting for him to check into his gate. Some of us were crying, and others looked like they were on the verge. We gave extra big hugs. As I embrace my brother and his long arms wrap all the way around me, I feel his magnificent love. Once the enfoldment was over, I couldn't help but feel this gnawing sense of impending doom. I knew it wouldn't be long before this love my brother and I shared would rip my heart in two. About an hour before his flight, he said his final goodbyes and rode the escalator up to his gate. Midway up, he looked back, and his eyes peered down, only to be met by ours, already watching him leave us. The look on his face said everything he didn't say when he was here. The things he is much too stoic to speak aloud. Although they are buried deep within his heart. I knew my brother was afraid of dying. It was such a big elephant it nearly squashes everyone in the room. He had probably been lying to himself about it. Smashing each frightening thought as it enters his mind. Not allowing himself to truly "feel" anything. That is my brother. He keeps his head down and gets the job done. Although he never applied for this position of death and dying. It was rudely handed to him, and he had no choice of whether or not to accept it.

# FACING IT

Cancer sucks.

Soon after Mike had left, Savannah began a job at Avera, one of our two local hospitals. Isaac began taking satellite classes at our local University Center. It was nice to have him home another year, and it saves him a ton of money on dorm, food, and activity fees.

I continue to futilely fight these demons that hold onto me so tightly. I can hear their whispers, encouraging me to perform horrendous acts upon myself. I can feel their sharp claws against my tender skin as I physically react to their presence. My pulse quickens. Beads of sweat fill my hairline and forehead. With each shallow breath, I try to defend myself against their piercing tones. It is no use. They have won before the battle even began. Without hesitation, I grab my hidden tools and lay them out in their routine sterile positioning on the bathroom counter as I lock the door behind me. The demons wrap themselves soundly around me as I stand before the bathroom mirror, with my kryptonite. I insert it into the right side of my nose. Blood squirts out like a large projectile and splatters the mirror with its red stain. Now, I can feel the point of the sharp scissors within my nasal canal. I continue to turn the instrument around and around, making the cut wider with jagged edges. I wanted to hurt myself. I deserved it. I cut to create the face that I saw in the mirror every morning before that first urge took over my life. I've always seen myself as scarred, open, and bleeding.

"Now the world is able to see the real me in the face that I have sculpted." My thoughts go to their darkest place, as the incessant blood will not clot, damming the river running from the fresh wound through my nose. "I despise the woman I have become. I wish I could simply wash her away."

Tim's reaction does not surprise me. "But you were doing so good. Why would you do this again? What is wrong with you?" His chatter only annoys me now. I had become so accustomed to it. A lot like getting punched in the gut. Eventually, you build up those abdominal muscles, so the impact of the hit is severely diminished. I had become virtually immune to his harshness. At least, that's what I told myself.

Nearly every day, after everybody had left the house for work or school, I would cut or jab. I would rip or pull. My flesh became my war zone. Me against them, and they were winning by a long shot. I had now severed the entire right side of my nostril. It is cut in two and open to my sinuses. The blood refuses to stop flowing, and at this point, I could care less. I slide my emaciated body down the blood-soaked bathroom wall in complete retreat, as I have no fight left in me.

Early that November, we received word that Mike was not doing well. I immediately booked tickets for my mom, my sister Michelle, Savannah, and myself, leaving the next day. During the flight to Michigan, my thoughts dug up cherished memories. He had told us in previous conversations, 'Love is stronger than death.' Was this what I was going to see? My 56-year-old brother die before my grief-filled eyes. Two medium-sized Band-Aids covered my nose, while another one right below covered my absent lip. I was embarrassed that my brother would have to see me so bandaged, so broken. I longed for him to be proud of me. Not to be afraid of this vicious monster within me. Our flight had so many delays we didn't arrive in Michigan until sundown. As we walked up the snowy driveway, my heart tore in the fear that his wife would open the door only to tell us that he had already passed. But that's not what happened. Instead, she opened the door, and without a word being spoken, I burst through it. I rushed over to the hospital bed that my dying brother was lying on. As he raised his arm for a hug, I could see how emaciated his body had become. His skin hung on the bones beneath, every bump and nodule visible through his thin flesh. He tried to talk, but his tongue was too dry and had stuck to the top of his mouth, making his words inaudible. His pain was no longer subjective. His anguish had become visible to the naked eye. My mind wondered how long he had been suffering. Instead of asking the question, I kept my attention focused on the small slice of time I had left with my brother. I desperately wanted to take him in my arms and hug him, but Melissa had instructed me that he was in too much pain to even be touched. I let all my weight fall on the bed rail and talked to my brother for the last time. At death's door, I finally told him all the things I should have shared with him throughout our years together. We were both vagabonds, battle buddies. This wonderful man that I served with in this war we all call life was now down and fatally wounded. No medic could save him. No treatment would allow him one more minute of life. After softly speaking to him for about an hour, I noticed a distinct change in his breathing. And he was gone within minutes. Like how the fuck does this happen? After he had let out his last breath, I screamed in grief and agony. I would not be consoled. I fought to lower the bed rail. Although I was unable to hold him just one hour ago, I can hold him now. So I did. I put each of my hands behind his shoulders, and lifted his limp, lifeless body for an embrace that would have to hold me for a lifetime.

My mind and spirit did not comprehend what the hell just happened. How can he be here until he's not? I hated it. I hated cancer. I hated life. I hated that I had held myself back with him because of this fucking disorder in my brain that makes me maul my face daily. I mean, jeez WTF? The guilt was laying heavy on my heart of all those special times we could have had if only I was normal. But that was a word I couldn't even define.

On our Uber ride home that night, not a word was spoken. Even in the silence, the absence of peace screamed out. As our driver pulled into the parking lot of our hotel, I questioned her on the availability of weed, as it was legal in Michigan. She told me she would hook me up and returned soon with four joints containing a drug that I needed to numb my emotions. I have never been high before, but I knew it would be better than hurting myself with my freshly embedded despair.

My daughter and I hid behind a large garbage dumpster to stay out of the cold Michigan breeze. Together, we finished the joint. I understood why they called it high because it sort of feels like an out-of-body experience. After what seemed to be a greater trek back to our hotel room, we crashed on the two queen size beds. Even being that high, I wanted to keep my eye on my, (also high) daughter. My mama bear instincts remained intact. Every few minutes, I would call over to her, "Are you all right, Savannah?" She would always assure me with an immediate "Yes." As she lay motionless on the bed next to me with her eyes closed. While the marijuana mixed with my ongoing thoughts of bereavement, I continually asked Michelle and my mom, "Did Mike really just die?" and, "Am I dead?" I could sense their annoyance, but that didn't stop me from asking those same two questions incessantly. My brain virtually could not begin to comprehend what had just occurred. But I was pretty sure I just lost my person forever.

Michelle changed our airline tickets so that we could fly out the next day. There was no point in staying. It was finished. Complete. His dash has been lived from 1962-2019. Too short of a life for such a strong, humble man.

Upon returning home, I questioned every detail about life and death, heaven and hell. I wanted to know how to pinpoint my brother's location. Is heaven on a different plane, making it invisible to us? Is it more like a chasm where we cannot see him, and his vision of us is blocked as well? I would search scripture for answers, finding that it left me with more inquiries than I had started with. While attending church, I listened to the saving grace of our Lord and the twelve different names of our God, all with a special meaning... The words blurred into my eardrums as my thoughts floated elsewhere. It was during these times, while I could hear His precious Word being read aloud, that my face would feel flush, and those all too familiar drops were formed in the base of my eyelid. I wanted to interrupt the sermon. To burst right up out of my chair and beg someone to tell me where my brother is. It is an awful feeling. I knew he was with God in heaven. My faith was not shaken. I wanted to be the Christopher Columbus of heaven. Discovering its location and thereby reassuring everyone with lost loved ones. But, most importantly, I longed to understand how it all works. Death happens in less than a second, in "the blink of an eye." What exactly happened to my brother's spirit in that moment, and where is he now? These questions plagued my soul.

I would still text him until Melissa disconnected his phone. Mike: When I watched you exhale your last breath of life, I experienced a spiritual heart attack, in a sense. It feels like the dead part of my heart is the place you used to fill. Time will not heal me or make things better. The more time I have, the more memories I recall, and saltier teardrops roll down my already moistened face. I hate that you are gone. Nearly four weeks have passed. I wonder how much time has passed for you. I don't mean to be selfish. I'm so glad your pain has stopped. I wish you had never been diagnosed with that fucking cancer. I tried to fight it, but like a brick wall, it only served to bloody my knuckles. I miss you so much, Mike. Please help me through.

Daily, I would awake in the early morning hours, mostly at 2 or 3 o'clock. I would sit hidden on that same garage stoop, sobbing over the pain of losing him. He was my big brother, my father figure, my protector. He was my person, and I feel hollow without him.

# Chapter 8

# The Battle Belongs to the Lord

Grieving my brother's death is an automatic response of being awake. I miss him more with each passing day and wish I could have one last moment with him now. But isn't that what everybody says who has lost a loved one? Why, as an intelligent society, don't we realize this phenomenon occurs with the loss of those that are important to us and learn from it? We would be an entirely different world, wouldn't we? Instead of being about the business of producing and purchasing, while filling our beautiful homes with tangible treasures, we would take advantage of every moment we have together. Irreplaceable portions of time would become our treasures. But, we relent to the peer pressure of society. Making death a clean getaway where no one stays hurting past the final burial. Such pure bullshit.

My heart physically aches from the pain induced the moment my brother left this world. Although we lived far apart, he visited often. I always knew he was there, in Michigan, just nine digits away from hearing his voice. Now I endlessly listen to the three voicemails I have saved from him. I never want to forget the sound of his voice. I never want to forget his face and his oversized, hard-working hands. I never want to stop grieving with tenacity. I fear if I do, Mike's memory will fade as my tear wells dry up.

# FACING IT

Needless to say, Christmas did not make the record books. I tried to look happy for my kids while we opened presents after our church's Christmas Eve Service. Another Walter tradition. I would have little sparks of what felt like joy, but no fire was lit that precious celebration on the Eve of our Savior's birth. It was sad for all of us. We all felt the vacancy in our hearts. Mine felt entirely empty.

I saw my first robin today. Spring has sprung. I can see the perennials pushing through the newly unfrozen ground. Large canopies are being built outside of various stores, soon to be filled with budding flowers and vegetable plants for the garden. Although I love to see the freshly sprung flowers and winter birds of the south returning home, the onset of spring makes me feel indifferent. I'm not ready for the beautiful trees lining their branches with different shades of green. I do not feel like the pretty monarch who has broken free from its snug cocoon. My ears try not to enjoy the harmonious melody all the birds make together just before the sun is about to rise. It's as if they are telling the world, "Wake up and see the sky our Creator has painted for us today. It is almost time for the big reveal." Sometimes I think birds' IQ may be higher than humans with the important stuff. We work so hard to build our kingdoms, just to be washed away by the incoming tide. Birds trust their instincts and always travel in groups. They sing a new song every morning with boastful glee, like an orchestrated symphony. They hunt for food when they are hungry and never worry if a feather is out of place. Smart.

As I dealt with the ongoing loss of my person, my confidant, my big brother and my protector, sorrow devours my days. I don't know what the hell I am supposed to do with myself. I can't wipe my face fast enough to dry it as my tears have transformed into a constant stream rolling down my cheeks. I have retreated because of my grief. It was so easy to isolate myself in 2020, the year everyone was sequestered to their homes. The COVID virus had reared its ugly head, shutting down unnecessary stores and mandating people to stay safe at home as much as possible. Easy. In my ever-deepening depression, I have no desire to see others and, in turn, have them see me. So I stayed at our house for twelve straight months. I would move so little. From my bed to the chair in the living room. At the end of the day, I would walk this long, marathonic distance back to my bed. I wouldn't even turn on the television. It annoyed me. I wanted to be alone with my dark thoughts encompassing me.

During this time, I quit attending Rustic Hills Church altogether. My friends would visit my hollowed soul. Bringing me flowers, homemade food and cards. Without fail, every week, I received a couple of letters of encouragement in the mail from my brothers and sisters in Christ. These notes meant so much to me. They made me feel wanted, albeit I was not ready to go to church and reveal my new bandages and scars to the entire congregation. I was lost in grief and trapped by my own misery.

I finally smelled fresh air, stepping outside for the first time in months. Once the spring rains gave way to flowers in full bloom, summer came upon us. Isaac is able to take a well-deserved break from his studies. This is the year that his girlfriend Maiya moved in with us, mostly due to her financial situation but also because she and Isaac are in love. It did my broken heart good to see my son so content with his life. They would fluently sit together and talk. I could hear her infectious laughter often throughout their conversation. It made me smile as its remnants filled our hallway. Savannah has been transferred to a better job at Avera Home Health with better pay and full benefits. I know she was glad to be done with her previous position, and working from home was a bonus. No travel time and save gas money. Nice. Tim continues working as a locksmith. My steady, never changing Rock of Gibraltar. While I remain my usual emotional mess with no job and, currently, no foresight for my future. I was in limbo.

I can see the leaves boasting their bright colors of autumn through our large picture window from my seat in our living room. Savannah, working from home, had been watching me let my sadness overtake my days. She knew I loved the ocean, and unbeknownst to me, she had been strolling through different websites to find the best deal for a vacation package to Miami South beach. Because of COVID, flying had hit an all-time low price, as

149

the airlines were struggling to fill their infinite empty seats. She showed me the printout of a particularly attractive hotel and resort, virtually on the beach. After glancing at the itinerary, Savannah asked me, "Shall I book it for us, Momma?" Without hesitation, I immediately answer with an excited, "Yes!" It surprised me to hear my voice spike with any emotion. I was excited. I desperately needed a change of scenery. Watching the seasons pass through this large picture window is only making my life less desirable.

We booked an entire week in the warm sun of Florida. In early October, we flew to our city of destination. Arriving late, we checked into the hotel and had a couple of drinks at the outside patio restaurant next door before turning in for the night. The next morning, we both awoke with great anticipation of relaxing at the beach. We ate our hotel's complimentary breakfast, which consisted of fresh fruit, biscuits, french toast, finger sandwiches and anything else our hearts could desire. It felt good to be eating this healthy. I felt invigorated as we walked down the sandy beach to the waters in full tide. A young man met us to set up our lounge chairs. He also dug the base of a large, yellow umbrella into the sand, giving shade to both Savannah and I. But we were much too busy delightfully enjoying the ocean waters, as the tide was in constant movement. It bounced us up and down and rocked our bodies back and forth in the chest-deep waters. Because my wounds have healed in a most undesirable way, I remain fully bandaged. Because of the large opening where flesh is supposed to be, I am unable to swim underwater. The ocean would fill my lungs as it flooded my open nasal cavity.

Unfortunately, I was unable to plunge into the waters headfirst like I would have liked to. Savannah, however, could dive into the waves to the sands below in search of the sought-after conch shell. I am smiling. I absolutely love the ocean, and the company I shared it with made it simply superb. We let the tide wash in, as our hands randomly grabbed whatever they could hold before the waters were thrust back into the deep ocean. We found a lot of sand and coral. Although, we did find some small, impressive seashells that we would later carefully wrap up for our flight home. Memoirs of a great day. After two days of soaking up the heat oceanside, we were sunburnt and suffering from heat exhaustion. We both needed to take a break from the heat and humidity, so the following day we adventured to Little Havana. This is where we enjoyed our first cup of real Cuban Coffee. Deliciously smooth. We visited several stores and sights before returning to our nicely air-conditioned hotel. Our legs were tired, but our spirits were endless. We finished our day by sitting in the sand, side by side, as we watched the sun's descent from its place on high to the clear, blue ocean on the distant horizon.

Colors of pink, yellow, purple and orange encircled the evening sky as the sun falls into the ocean to sleep until morning. That next night, we wanted to experience the true taste of seafood fresh from the ocean. We asked our Lyft driver for the name of a good seafood restaurant, and he dropped us off in Little Italy, bustling with restaurants and entertainment galore. We strolled along the alleyway as lights strung above our heads burned bright in the dark night. We decided on a corner restaurant that looked fancy and boasted of its fresh seafood. As our flaming dinner platter was delivered to our table, I saw two lobster eyes staring back at me. Normally, I would have been totally grossed out, but this was vacation. As we broke the lobster's shell and heard the loud "Crack!" we both giggled. Neither of us have had food like this before. We come from cattle country. A whole new experience for our palates. The humongous shrimp looked like it had just walked out of the ocean. I peeled its skin back and savored its enticing flavor. There was also some special kind of fish on this platter, with its head still attached, of course. That night, Savannah and I put away our limiting reservations. We cracked the lobster and peeled the shrimp. We flaked the fish, leaving its scaly skin on the plate. We were embarking on a new land with different sights, sounds and tastes. And I was thoroughly enjoying every moment I spent with my daughter on the adventure she had booked for us. Returning home was bittersweet. I had missed Tim and Isaac immensely, and I enjoyed sharing every detail about our experiences with them. Yet my heart longed to feel the ocean breeze against my skin one more time. To swim in the salty waters and be warmed by the heat of the

# FACING IT

Floridian sun. It was the trip of a lifetime. One I will not soon forget.

I finally made the brave decision to celebrate Thanksgiving with Tim's side of the family. My pretending was over. The time had come for me to crawl out of the cave I had been hiding in. I have grown weary from the cold darkness. I feel naked and vulnerable as I enter the house, already bustling with my relatives. A wave of sheer fear courses through my body. I am afraid of the looks of disgrace, the gasps of disbelief and the utter disgust my family will feel for me. How dare I show up to such a gathering? I know that eating Thanksgiving dinner with them will be challenging, as food falls from my mouth and stains my dress. My heap of napkins growing larger with each bite. My nose and upper lip are heavily bandaged, and no one knows what lies underneath. No one. I am in utter shock over my family's love and acceptance. Nobody questions my bandages or mentions my absence from their lives for the last several months. I am only met with hugs and greetings of recognition. My dinner is filled with welcoming and fulfilling fellowship with my family. I listen to each individual word with earnestness, trying to catch up on what's happening with everyone. I am so glad I came. I wished I hadn't stayed hidden so long within my deep grief and depression. Betty said to me privately, "I am so proud of you for coming today." That meant a lot to me. The validation of the brave woman I have just become. "Thud. Crack!" Weird feeling. I haven't felt it in such a long time. I barely

153

recognized it.

Bricks fell from the oversized wall that I have been building higher throughout my past twenty years of doctors, psychiatrists, specialists and counselors. This shield is around the place within my soul that contains every emotion I possess. I think within my head, but I feel within my heart. This is my organ in need of protection. So many bricks were laid to shield me from my relentless shame and guilt. Because of their tenacity, both found ways of seeping in through the barrier I had created. Sometimes the pressure almost made my heart burst into a million pieces. And all the king's horses and all the king's men would not have been able to put me together again. But this night has brought me love and acceptance. Tim helps me with my winter coat as we all give hugs and say our goodbyes. On the ride home that special night, I relived the entirety of the evening within the walls of my mind.

I fearfully entered the party, 'dead man walking'. As I was leaving, I stepped across the threshold of the doorway to a new beginning. As I walked down the wooden porch stairs, God was seeing the first few steps of a new life. He knows my entire timeline, albeit I am only allowed to experience the moment at hand. God knows my soul, and he will never give me too much to bear. Slices of time are what my mind and body can barely handle.

It is Christmas Eve 2020. I begin to change the many

bandages on my face. I also apply makeup and put on a festive dress. The entire time I am getting ready, I am not sure that I will be going. Tim catches a glimpse of me in the mirror, applying lipstick on my remaining lower lip and encourages me to come with them. I take his advice. My first time back at church in several months. I am struck with anxiety as my hand reaches for the handle of the double doors leading into our fellowship hall. "What will they say? Will everyone be staring at my newly chiseled face?" Upon entering, I am immediately greeted by Dianne. She is a tiny lady, about 30 years my senior. With wide open arms, she welcomes me. I am drawn to her warmth as we embrace. She was my friend who would write to me every week without fail. I had just received a letter from her a couple of days ago, which is what finally prompted me to attend church tonight. I thought, "These people will never give up on me. I might as well just go and show them my shame-filled face." Once again, I was overwhelmed by people's graciousness. Nobody stared or said one word about the new bandages covering the entirety of my nose. I was met with love and thanksgiving. I felt like the prodigal son returning home. It was a beautiful candlelight service, and I left with my spirits lifted. We had a great Christmas that year. Although a conservative gift-giving holiday, we all did remember the reason for the season. Jesus had always had a hold of my heart, and now, I was searching for a deeper relationship with Him.

Winter's blistering cold weather has subsided, and the snow

heaps have all melted. It is a beautiful spring day as I sit outside on the front steps of our porch. Fully bandaged and scarred face in full view of all my neighbors who are also outside, enjoying the nice day. I am happy. Happy because I can see the sun sparkling across my face as the leaves from the trees are tossed about by the warm breeze. Happy because I have a loving family who accepts me for who I am. Scars and all. Happy because I have found a tiny spark of hope within me. The fire has been burnt out for so long, yet there it was. A bright, glittery spark. It was something. I clutched onto it with every fiber of my being.

By this time, I had set up a meeting with a lawyer that Tim attended high school with. David King. The name sounds so prominent and intimidating. I met this short, overweight, balding shirt-and-tie guy. I feel better. His name does not match his stature. We sat down in his office to discuss applying for disability. I tell him my story in a nutshell, and he tries to keep an expressionless face. He did not succeed. His assistant gasps as she covers her wide-open mouth. I also failed at remaining expressionless and feel tears well up in my eyes. As one drops to the floor, David hands me the Kleenex as he nods towards the box as if to say, "Take one. I have no idea what else to do. My brain is exploding." I gave them all of my life's truths within an hour of time. It was purely visible that they were both shaken and overwhelmed, desperately wanting to run screaming out of that office. But they remained in their appropriate, stoic, business-like personas that had been instilled in them throughout their training and careers. She takes notes as David explains the process. I signed several pages giving him full access to all of my doctors. This allows him permission to view every word ever recorded throughout my many visits. He is permitted to examine the before pictures of each of my surgeries. But it was time. Time to trust someone for no other reason than my husband told me that in high school, he was a good guy.

The day that David has been feverishly preparing for is finally upon us. He looks confident as we climb the stairs to the courthouse for my disability request hearing. As we walk into the courtroom, I see the judge's head turn quickly in my direction. His eyes meet mine, and I instantly lower my head to the floor. I am full of shame. I have bandages covering my entire nose, encompassing my chin, and jacketing my absent upper lip. I can feel his constant stare burn a hole through the top of my skull as I refuse to look up and meet his gaze. I know he thinks I am full-blown crazy. I sat down next to David. He tells the judge some physical things I had wrong with me. I had recently been diagnosed with degenerative disk disease, making every move more difficult. Walking brings fire to my lower back, shooting through my right leg. I am also constantly anemic. My red blood cells have begun destroying themselves, making me tired virtually all the time. My body is unable to absorb iron through my digestive system, so I have infusions every three weeks or so. The judge respectably listens to what David is saying, but after several minutes, he grows weary of my list of physical ailments and stops David with a motion of his hand. "Now, I think we need to dig deeper here. Let's have her see our court psychiatrist." David then unexpectedly asks me to leave the courtroom and invites Tim inside. Now I am sitting in the waiting area in place of my husband. "What is going on in there? Why would David do that?" I felt betrayed that he had not told me beforehand that it was his intention for my husband and I to trade places. Finally, David and Tim exited the courtroom together. David told me he would be calling me with the details of my appointment with the state psychiatrist. "Great. Wonderful." I immediately asked Tim what had happened during my long absence. He briefly summarizes it for me. "David wanted me to tell the judge of all that you had been through in your past that has brought you to where you are today." My tender-hearted lawyer wanted to tell the judge some of the ghosts from my past that he was overloaded with on that first day we met. He didn't want me to be burdened with reliving them again, so he had secretly let Tim know before our court date what he would be asking of him. "Wow." His compassion astounds me. He has a sensitive heart that has tenderly held the heart of this broken bird in his hands. David protected me. "Thud. Kerplunk." "Regular people may be okay with me even when they know my story? Unbelievable." I thought to myself as I slipped into the passenger seat and left the courthouse.

I talked for two hours with the court's state psychiatrist. The only time I spoke was to answer each of her many questions. Every reply prompts another inquiry into my life. I left her office emotionally exhausted. Once again, I was forced to tell truths that I wanted to keep hidden. Leaving her office, I felt unsure of how this session would help me get the assistance I needed. I drove home in tears.

A couple of weeks later, David and I once again made our way up the stairs to the courthouse for the decision the judge has made regarding my disability. I anxiously entered the courtroom, already averting the eyes of the judge. He talked about some legal jargon and dismissed us. There was sensitivity in his eyes as he spoke. I didn't have to say a word. I also had no idea what had just happened. David and I walked towards my van as he explained to me that the judge had just awarded me full disability with healthcare insurance available to me at a reduced rate. Elation filled my veins. This arduous process was complete, and I would soon be receiving assistance each month to help my family financially. David worked so hard for me, and I am forever grateful.

As we replace our calendars to the year of 2021, COVID remains alive and well throughout our nation. Although the unnecessary stores have been allowed to reopen, masks were still required everywhere, and shoppers were strongly encouraged to keep a six-foot distance from each other as much as possible. For the most part, people were glad to be able to leave their homes again. Parents were overjoyed that public schools had reopened. The virus was still present, but the fight against it had simmered down to a tolerable level.

South Dakotans had voted for the implementation of medical marijuana. It didn't take me long to acquire a medical marijuana card. My husband could see how much it was helping me and didn't mind the one-hour drive to the only dispensary open so that I could obtain my herbal medicine. It took me a while to learn how to become comfortably high. Just high enough to kill the pain while reclaiming my wits about me. Marijuana, whether smoked or ingested, makes me think about everything. The past and all that it held within it and the future I didn't think I would have. It made me easier to get along with because I saw things more clearly, and found that the little stuff really doesn't matter. I was in constant communication with my Lord regarding my new medicine. I did not want to be participating in something he did not approve of.

So my life continued. Then I noticed something so very different one particular day. I noticed that I hadn't had that intense urge to hurt myself for several weeks. My nose and upper lip bandages remained intact due to the disfigurement that lies beneath, but I have had no new slices taken from my flesh. I had become so accustomed to my daily struggles I could not believe I hadn't noticed it sooner. It's kind of like when I get a bad headache. If I become engaged in something that would transfer my mind's attention, my headache would disappear without me even noticing. My amnesia would end at some distant, random point in time, and I could never believe that the absence of my great head pain went unnoticed. This was similar but on a much, much grander scale.

I was afraid to tell people, just in case that great urge returned, and I once again became powerless over it. So I continued living my normal routine. I am up early in the morning, usually around two o'clock. I immediately start the coffee brewing before I do anything else. An insomniac's best friend while everyone else lies sleeping. I had to learn how to live again. Hurting myself had taken up all my spare time in the past. I sat, sipping my warm, cream-filled coffee, while I searched my brain for quiet activities that I could entertain myself with until the rest of my family would be waking up. Their routine alarm is around 7 am, several hours from my abnormal internal clock, giving me a good five hours to spend alone each morning. At first, I felt intimidated at the mountain of time I had to fill before seeing a live human being. Nothing good has happened from my alone time in the past. After much soul-searching, I came to enjoy these hours I had to myself. I was awake before the precious sparrows that I have been feeding regularly for several years. They depend on me. I have two large bird feeders and two smaller ones that my kiddos made when they were little. They have screws holding the old, weathered wood together, and red paracord have replaced their wooden perches, as the wood simply crumbled from the weather changes it has had to endure over the past twenty years. I am a very nostalgic person. I love being able to sit on my front porch, just as the sun is rising, and watch my precious birds as their chirps and chatter fill the air of the breaking dawn. They perch on their makeshift paracord branch, eating from the bird feeders made by the small hands of my children. Priceless indeed.

During this early morning alone time, I rediscovered my love of music. Listening to Christian songs feed my soul. The melodies went in through my eardrums with a straight jetline for my heart. It was when I was enveloped with worship music that I felt closest to God. There is something so powerful about music. Anyone who has physically felt the bass of a loud song playing within their chest walls can relate to the sensation that I am trying to convey. When you mix the Gospel message with that music, it can be life-altering. And for me, it was.

The songs constantly streamed into my ears via Bluetooth headphones as I would draw the images in my mind's eye. With paper and pencil, I would record sketches of last night's nightmare or thoughts of my past depression. I noticed as time passed that my drawings were becoming more uplifting. I would sketch pictures of people I knew or scenery from a place I had recently visited. My entire sketchbook was filled with images from my mind. In the past, those dark images would haunt me. It's as if by transferring them with paper and pencil, I was able to blur the lines in my mind a bit, bringing me great peace.

So every morning, I ignored whatever time my IPhone read and arose from bed when I felt awake. I would sit at our dining room table, listening to my gospel music, while I enhanced my drawing abilities. The rest of my family remained asleep in their beds, dreams filling their slumber. Tim and Savannah were usually the first to awaken, soon to be followed by Isaac and Maiya. We would sit at our kitchen table enjoying the fresh brewed coffee while the conversation flowed with ease. I was always interested in how they slept and what they dreamt about. I would question what they did last night while I lay sleeping. Because of my current circadian rhythm and constant low blood iron, I would grow weary early in the evening. Usually, I would be in bed before Tim returned home from work. This was a difficult time, because of the infinite hours I spent alone. I was living a separate life from that of my family. Tim and I only had about an hour in the morning together. Our opposing sleep schedule made our time a precious commodity even more than usual because of its rarity.

I knew God, and I were on a journey together. I leaned on Him continually as I searched His Heart through song and scripture. I knew He is my Savior. He has saved me from the depths of the waters and from the great stain of my sins. I have found through my many trials in life Jesus was right there, whispering in my ear, "Follow Me." Through my darkest valley, when I felt cold and alone as I lay on the operating room table for another surgical revision of my face, I would hide in the shadow of His Presence. He would reassure me, "Have faith, my child. I will lead you through the bramble. Your outer man may be suffering, but your inner man is being renewed day by day. Put one foot in front of the other, and step by step, Follow Me." As I lay badly wounded and in pain from the dark depression that consumed me, He would ask me, "Do you want to be made well? Follow me."

When I stumbled, He would help me regain my composure. When I tripped and fell on the path, He graciously helped me ground my footing. "I am right here with you always. Fight the good fight, and keep running your race. I will be a lamp unto your feet and a light unto your path. Follow me." When barely gripping onto the edge of a cliff, the ghosts from my past tugging at my dangling legs as I look to the abyss below, He would raise me up onto the solid rock where I could stand. He would warm me with His presence and remind me, "I am here with you. Do not be afraid. Follow me." Even in agony, frustration and anger as I would throw my fists to the heavens. He would softly whisper, "Be still and know that I am enough. Follow me." As I would crumble underneath the weight of my guilt and shame born from my sins and the sins committed against me, He would lift me up and support me with His saving grace. "I have cleansed you with my blood. Scarlet has washed you white as snow. You are holy in My eyes. Follow me." So I did. I placed my hand in His, and I followed Him with pure humility and humbleness of heart.

Because of my relationship with the Lord, I find myself in His scripture virtually daily. I can distinctly relate to different people in the bible. The lowly of heart that Jesus somehow incorporates into His short life here on this earth. I can see myself there as the humble man approaches the temple. Because of his intense remorse, he is unable to hold his head up and stands in the distance, thinking his sins are too many. He beats his chest and calls out to God in repentance. That extreme feeling of shame and guilt is something I can empathize with.

Of all the bible characters, I can fully relate to Mary Magdalene. When Mary first met Jesus, she was about to be stoned for adultery. Instead, Jesus told the crowd, "Whoever is without sin, let him cast the first stone." He pauses before kneeling down in the dirt and making each, and every one of her accusers watch as he wrote all of their sins on the dusty ground laid before them. As each 'righteous' man saw his sin, he walked away, dropping his stone by her feet. Then it was just her and Jesus. She did not ask forgiveness, nor did she prepare a burnt offering before God. Yet Jesus did not condemn her and told her to go and sin no more. From that moment on, Mary followed Jesus all the way to Calvary. For those who are forgiven much, love much. She sat at her Lord's feet, her sister Martha upset with her for not helping prepare the dinner. This defines my very being. I would choose Jesus.

Have you ever thought about how Mary reacted when Jesus showed up four days after her brother, Lazarus, had passed away? Although they had sent word to Him, He did not rush to their house. Instead, He took a two-day pause before beginning the journey to Bethany, where they lived. Her sister Martha met Him at the city's gate, while Mary stayed back at their home. Once Jesus calls for Mary, she comes quickly and falls at his feet, pleading with Him in her grief, "Lord, if You had been here, my brother would not have died." I can relate to her feelings of distress, as I have been indignant with the Lord when He has not promptly answered my pleading and prayers. Similar to Mary, it is hard for me to see that His ways are not our ways.

On that grief-filled day, Mary could not have known that Lazarus' death would be utilized for God's Glory. How stunned she must have been when Jesus called Lazarus back to life. "Let not your heart be troubled; you believe in God, believe also in me." Not long after this, Jesus was the guest of honor at a dinner feast at their house, with Lazarus present at the table. Mary took an extremely expensive pint of perfume and poured it on Jesus' feet, and wiped them with her hair as she wept. I can only imagine the intense emotions she was having during this time. It is too profound to explain with mere words. I know she loved Him with her mind, body and soul and would follow Him anywhere. Although a vagabond, Jesus redeemed her. She was present for His crucifixion, as He was virtually unrecognizable from the beatings and scourging he had to endure before being nailed to a tree. Three days later, when she went to the tomb with spices in hand, He chose to share The Good News with her first. "He is not here, but is risen." declares the Angel of the Lord to His humble servant who loves Him much.

The bible is full of priceless treasures, much like the pearl that the man sold his entire field for. It held so much value, it was worth all he had. The line is open with God at all hours. Our early morning talks became routine. I would tell Him all I was thankful for and pray for continued healing for my entire family. I conversed with Him as if He were sitting with me, sipping coffee, as we simply talk with one another. He is my Papa and longs to hear about my life. It is similar to how I feel as a mother. I can see my children living their lives around me. But, it is when they take the time to sit down and genuinely talk with me face to face, that I feel closest to them. When they share the news of their daily life experiences with me, I feel worthwhile. They love me enough to take their precious time and give it to me. If time were tangible, they would be handing me a present box wrapped in shiny gold paper with a big, red bow. And inside would be that pearl.

# Chapter 9
# Yahweh-Rophe (The Lord Heals)

As the hands of the clock keep ticking along, day by day, I continue waking up hours before my family. In this time alone, I read scripture. I can feel God's Word being spoken directly to my soul. I suppose that's why they call it The Living Word. Although I have read the bible several times, He talks with me through His Word. He meets me here, right where I am. Sitting at my kitchen table in the darkness of these hours before He makes our sunrise, bringing first light to the day ahead. In the Christian music that fills my ears, I listen to Gospel truths spoken to my heart in a most harmonious way. This is a journey I began when my brother died. It was then that I found myself in scripture daily, reading every verse about death and dying, heaven and hell. Although I found it impossible to pinpoint the exact location of my brother's soul, somewhere in my diligent searches, I found peace about him going home. That doesn't mean I miss him any less. Quite the contrary.

As he exhaled life's last breath, this world somehow changed for me. It feels peculiar without him in it. The Lord has comforted my grief, allowing me to move forward with my life, albeit the pace is quite slow. I no longer hide on the stoop in our garage, sobbing until it is hard to breathe. The vastness of the grieving process has several stages. I am glad to be over the endless hours of crying while thoughts of Mike constantly flash in my mind. When I remember him now, it may make my eyes well up with tears or bring a smile to my face. I sometimes laugh as I recall a funny episode of his impromptu shenanigans. It felt wonderful to have the peace only the Lord can give. He gives not as the world gives. His gifts are everlasting. The peace of The Lord was always available to me. The day I learned to accept it, a transformation occurred. My mind, body and soul was filled with a peace that surpasses understanding. With each recurring day, no matter the circumstances, my peace remains. I still do not understand His ways, but I trust His unshakable love and all that is contained within it. He is patient with me. He is kind. He does not judge me but glorifies at my accomplishments. His love is everlasting, just as the peace buried deep within my soul.

Every day I wake up, read my bible, listen to Christian music, and revisit my drawing abilities. This became extremely therapeutic for me. I was using my hands in a productive way. Creating a scene from within the walls of my mind with mere paper and pencil. It was in these early morning hours that He met me in an entirely new way. He became My Counselor, working through the whirling thoughts within the confines of my mind. He made me see how much anxiety-producing energy I was expending, letting the past keep a hold of me. He taught me to acknowledge the pain and the hurt caused by me and by others. I had such a long list of grievances. My hurt, anger and bitterness have hardened my heart. I lived in fear of rejection. I didn't want to see disgrace in people's eyes any longer. I had grown tired of the life I had created for myself. I met His nudges, encouraging me to forgive, with anger and regret still residing within my heart. "How can You expect me to let go of the atrocities done to my body? My brain has become fractured because of all my past wounds. Now I am supposed to simply let them go?"

I cried out to Him with despair. "Yes." I heard the gentle whisper of my Lord. He held my hand and led me through the embryonic stage of my forgiveness. I desperately desired freedom from the old, rusted chains of anger and animosity. I discovered, much like following Christ, it is a daily process. I said the prayer. I forgave the persons and all the ugliness they had brought upon me. My heart felt light. Ten minutes later, it returned to its previous hardened state as the memories flooded my mind. Each one is worse than the last, making me need to forgive them all over again. But I didn't. Not right away, anyway. I discovered that forgiveness is a long, formidable process.

Nevertheless, I felt devoted to running the distance and reaching freedom from these chains that bind me. I started to make a list of the people I needed to forgive on scratch paper. I hesitantly scribble my name on the bottom, saving the most difficult task for last. This would take a miracle from God, as I still hated myself for the years I spent putting my family through hell. How could I ever give myself mercy? In the past, I was my own judge and executioner. "Forgiveness is not an event, but rather a process. Be patient, little one. I am healing you from the inside out." That all-too-familiar whisper restores my peace.

As the sands of time kept flowing, I found myself creating finished projects that I would show my family as they unduly complimented my 'magnificent' sketches. They have always cheered me on. I could have spent my entire morning drawing two stick people under a rainbow (one of my favorite pictures to draw as a child), and their reaction would have remained the same. Their souls were all content that God had unveiled a piece of joy hidden within the darkness that had consumed me. I could feel the light of the Holy Spirit alive in me once again. That spark that flickered so many months ago has become an everlasting light within my soul. I want to please my Lord. To be the person He intended me to be. Through life's trials, I had debunked my fantasy to be that perfect, white picket fence mom and wife. God had different plans for me. When we are truly broken, the Maker can take what we have smashed to pieces and sculpt it into a beautiful new being. It is never what I would have envisioned for my future, albeit it is much better than the life I was leading when I left my Lord locked up in a depository, rooted in the recesses of my heart.

Unfortunately, during this time, my blood's ability to bind itself to iron proved impossible. Although I had my infusions every three weeks, my labs were skewed with every test, and my body grew tired easily. These early morning hours have become the bulk of my day. I sometimes slept for days when my iron stores were plummeting, as it was nearing time for another infusion. This proved challenging to deal with, as it limited my family time to nearly nil. Spending time with my loved ones is so important to me. I missed them. Sleep was no substitution for the life I desired. I was still unaware of the journey that the Lord had begun in my path of life. One that would transform my very being.

One Saturday, early in March, as Tim and I were having our morning coffee together, he commented on how he had observed the absence of any cuts or lacerations the last few months. "I've noticed your face has looked clear lately." His statement sounded more like a question, so I replied. "Yeah, I haven't really had the urge lately." I held back on how well I had been doing. My hesitation was caused by the deep seeded fear that my urges would return and I would let everybody down again, as they fiercely inquired of me, "Why?" Tim continued our conversation. "How is it looking under your bandages?" I have never shown anyone what lies beneath. "It's completely healed, but it healed in such a way that I have severe disfigurement. So I continue to wear the bandages." Tim nods in acceptance of my answer, although I'm unsure if he believes me. And for the first time in my life, I don't care if he does. It's between me and God now, and He knows I am telling the truth.

# FACING IT

My early morning alone time with the Lord continued. I would talk with Him endlessly as my hands kept busy sketching, painting or sculpting different scenes or faces. Nearly every morning, upon first awakening, extreme anxiety plagued my soul, as ghosts from yesterday haunted me nightly. My psychiatrist had prescribed a medicine to help PTSD night terrors, to no avail. So each morning, my first cup of coffee was poured with a shaky hand as my nerves were frazzled by my past being replayed in my subconscious throughout the night. I found that these newly discovered hobbies brought much-needed mindfulness and helped calm my angst. Being engaged in my numerous projects steadied my hand and brought relief to my spirit. I believe now that it was all the Lord at work in my life. He allowed me to replace my self-mutilating behaviors with a new hobby that used my hands in an altogether different way. I breathe deeply and my pulse is at rest. There is no sweat over my brow and I feel the brewing storm within my bones calmed. I am allowed free time to speak to my Lord about anything that pops into my head. From a prayer request for a friend to a prayer of thanksgiving for my progress. I dialed His number as soon as I sat down at my kitchen table, and I kept Him on the line for hours, talking incessantly to Him within the walls of my mind. That is a great attribute of Our Lord. He can hear my thoughts, all of them. Whether I am actively speaking to Him or not. He knows my troubles. He has succumbed to the human condition. He visited

Earth to save our souls for all of eternity so that we may live out our endless days in paradise with Him. "What an awesome God we serve." I quietly think to myself as I sip lukewarm coffee through my straw.

This March came in like a lion, with snow drifts halfway up our doorway. It ended like a lamb. The sun shone brightly in the blue sky, scattered with puffy, white clouds. Isaac would soon be finishing his junior year of college and returning home for the summer, along with Maiya. Savannah continues working for Avera Healthcare in the comfort of our own home. We transformed Isaac's bedroom into an office for her and made a makeshift living area for Maiya and him on the lower level of our home. They spend the majority of their days upstairs, but it was nice for them to have their own space away from the rest of the world to take respite in Tim continues to work at Fred the Fixer, now past his 30-year mark. Every Sunday, we attend church together. I soak up the scripture like a nice Spring rain on the freshly tilled soil of my soul. We could all sense the change happening within our household. Our family stuck together through all the storms of our life. They knew it had to be a group effort. My people had my back, no matter how high the waters crashed against our well-worn boat with tattered sails. A cord of three strands is not easily broken. Although, I tested the durability of that rope several times, as my frayed strand would begin to break under the pressure I constantly exerted on it. The transformation of the Lord has just begun. And He who started a good work in me will carry it on to completion until the day of Christ Jesus.

As the welcomed warmer temperatures launched in anticipation of summer and the fresh sprouts gave bloom to splendid, brightly-colored flowers, I noticed a defined change in me. There was no question about it. God has been tilling the garden of my soul, as I received His word as sunshine for my spirit. Instead of defining myself with my grave disorder, I now feel embodied by God's never-ending love. This is who I am now. Loved by God. This has become my new identity. The Holy Spirit has become ablaze in me once again. I first noticed the distinct change on a routine trip to the grocery store. My face did not bow down in hopes of hiding my bandages. My eyes did not avert the stares of others. Instead, I met their gaze with a friendly smile. I felt this warm sensation overtake my body, as my mind was filled with awe and wonder. My hate for myself was diminishing as I could see how lovable I was through Christ's eyes. This is just the beginning of the total transformation my inner man would be experiencing throughout my journey with My Papa, My Lord.

My daughter suggested a three-day trip to the Omaha Zoo early that May. Another Walter Favorite. We drove the four hours with excitement for our well-deserved mini-vacation. Savannah and I went back and forth on which animals we would visit first. Our favorite was the aquarium, where you could walk under a tunnel of clear glass, making it possible to envision all the sea creatures contained within the larger-than-life-sized tank. It mystified all of our senses simultaneously. We quickly decided that we would visit that exhibit first. Did I mention it was Memorial Day weekend? Upon pulling into the parking lot of the zoo, we were alarmed at how busy it was. Our only option was to park our vehicle a couple of blocks away on a side street and walk to the entrance of the zoo. Once inside, we saw each building with extra long lines filled with families and strollers and crying babies. To avoid the chaotic scene, we meandered around the perimeter of the zoo, having fun just getting lost together. We enjoyed watching the seals give a spectacular performance, as their trainer would give them a treat for each trick they skillfully achieved. After a couple of hours, with extreme noise penetrating our eardrums and unsettling heat beating down on our worn-out bodies, we left the zoo. We made plans to return the next day when it would be less busy. Walking back to the car, I can feel a migraine pulsating over my left eye. We returned to our hotel to get cleaned up for a pleasant dinner in their marketplace district.

Downtown was ablaze with people. We found a seat at the bar, and both ordered a drink. I felt it would help my headache, as the ibuprofen felt like sugar pills for the intense pain. That first drink went down fast and smooth. It wasn't long before I had another in front of me. Savannah and I collectively made a pact that we would only consume two drinks just enough to take the edge off. We wanted to keep our wits about us, because after dinner, we intended to walk along the marketplace's paths and visit some of the interesting stores. The second drink went down just as smoothly and almost as quickly as the first. I was feeling no pain. But true to form, I seemed to have overdue my alcohol. I began thinking about when my drinking had started. I began drinking beer around age 12 up until I turned 21. Once I become of legal age, I put my partying days behind me. Tim and I were married. We both seriously contemplated becoming pregnant, so I stopped alcohol completely. Until Mike passed away, his death pulled the rug out from under me, and I found myself falling further into the abyss. Alcohol became my close companion once again. I found that it served to numb the pain of my brother's death. So here I sit, nearly two years after his passing, at the bar of a restaurant/lounge with my 24-year-old daughter. As I watch her slowly sip on her second drink, I order another. I liked to feel numb. Within its damaged walls, there was no pain and no memories

Just a drunken stupor. I drowned my third drink with the same tenacity as I had the first two. I would have ordered a fourth, but Savannah physically dragged me off my barstool. We walked around one of the stores, and Savannah bought a cute troll doll for her grandma. Unbeknownst to me, Savannah had already called for a Lyft to take us back to our hotel. I was mad at her. "Who the hell are you to tell me when it's time to go home? I want to go back to the bar." Savannah's reply was simple yet firm. "We are leaving." I sat on the curb like a toddler throwing a tantrum. Our car arrived, and as she opened the door, I fell into the back seat. My head was spinning from the strong drinks.

I woke up the next morning with an explosive migraine and nausea that felt like if I moved an inch, I might puke. We stayed at our hotel until they made us leave, around noon. During the long trek back to Sioux Falls, my mind travels through my long list of regrets. Most currently, ruining our special mini-vacation by drinking too much. I was thankful that Savannah pulled me off my barstool when she did. As I lay reclined in her passenger seat, the rumbling of the road beneath us made me feel sick. Savannah had to stop a couple of times so that I could throw up last night's despair. How embarrassing. I knew I screwed up, and I never wanted to be this disappointed in myself again.

After being home for a couple of days, Savannah and I engaged in a dialogue about my addictive behavior, which had reached its peak in Omaha, destroying our mini-vacation that we had both looked forward to. I had made a choice to end my use of alcohol during the horrendous four-hour drive home. Time that we had intended to spend at the zoo together. Alcohol does have a way of ruining the most precious moments in life, doesn't it? Together,

Savannah and I thought of creating a calendar, and each day that I would abstain from alcohol, I would draw a simple picture of activity within the day that I was able to participate in. An engagement of life that would have been stalled or even prevented by my alcoholism.

During this time of numbing myself from life's tragedies, I had let alcohol take over my life. When my emotions would start filling me with their intensity, I would grab a beer or, at times, mix Sprite and vodka. I would eagerly wait for the alcohol to reach my bloodstream until all my pent-up emotions seemed to disappear. Awakening the next morning, I would experience all those emotions I had just numbed the night before with a dollop of regret on top. Stupid. It bears saying again: I sometimes think my sparrows have more brains than I do. I fought to remain sober. I found myself daily going all twelve rounds within the confines of my mind.

The first two weeks were the hardest, with most of my calendar drawings showing how tough my day was in a picture format. It was during this time that I pleaded with the Lord to take away my great desire to feel nothing by using alcohol to replace my emotions. He heard my cry and saw my pain. He met me again right where I am. He listened patiently to my prayers for freedom from the clutches alcohol had over my life. I felt powerless by myself. However, I did realize I had the power within me to invite Christ into the ring to fight for me. We tag-teamed this great battle, with me standing on the side of the ring, watching in awe as the Lord fought my demons for me. I remained still in His Presence. After two weeks of sobriety, I rewarded myself with a simple five-dollar thrift store bracelet that I still wear to this day. It serves as a constant reminder of how far I've come and my promise to myself, my family and my Lord.

I noticed my overwhelming desire for a smooth drink to take the edge off had dissipated greatly. Every morning that I woke up from the previous day's sobriety, I would sketch a quick picture in my calendar. I noticed a distinct contrast in the pictures from the first two weeks versus the pictures I was presently sketching. Instead of a face with eyes exuded out, describing a hard day for me, my new sketches consisted of garage sailing with Isaac and making dinner with Savannah. So many things to rediscover as I slowly come out of my two-year alcohol-induced coma. I am tired of trying to do life on my own, always keeping Jesus at a distance. He became my Saviour from the spirits of alcoholism. It was a beast I could have never defeated on my own. Because I gave the Lord control over my life and its struggles, I have gained His power over my addiction. Releasing me from the clutches of alcoholism was one of the first steps in His plan of redemption for my life. It felt empowering to live life sober. With each passing day my existence became less difficult. I was off my tightrope between the darkness and the light. I had fallen into the precious grace of our Lord and

Savior. It was beautiful. The season's fresh flowers aroma filled my senses with a new joy. A joy that can only come from having Christ living within me. He never stopped chasing after me to fill the distance that I could never do. I was done settling for surviving the life that I futilely tried to pretend through. I longed to thrive through the life that can only come from freedom with Christ. I was ready to walk the path laid before me with the Holy Spirit ablaze within me.

One day, in late June, after being sober for over a month, Tim and I were sitting on our back deck, enjoying the coolness of the evening. We were chatting about our days and the subject somehow made it around to how I am jealous of him. He seemed normal to me and the rest of the world. He didn't have any grave mental disorder or suffer from lack of self-control like I did. He gave me a short list of his faults in an attempt to make me feel better about myself. "You do not have an addictive personality," I reassured him. "I'm addicted to you." was his only response. My sweet boy in the dark flannel shirt sat in front of me, and I could see him clearly through the 29 years that have passed since that first introduction. Tim has been present for me through every step of the dark path that I had taken us down. He would hold my hand and try to protect me from myself. Staying up endless hours to watch over me, ensuring I do not lock myself behind our atrocious bathroom door. He was all too familiar with what might happen. I often felt sorry for him as he would go to work the next morning with dark puffiness under his eyes. The kind of look that comes from little or no sleep, as life has thrust him through the gates of hell. Although he tried his best, he could not control this monster inside me any better than I could. It was never the scars that bothered me, as much as the shame of knowing that I had put them there.

That my body had a monster within it that no doctor, medicine, counseling or pure will could destroy. It refused to stop. Oh, but how he tried. He was there at the hospital, as I told my nurse to "Go to Hell." I concurrently proceeded to curse every staff member that dared to enter my hospital room. I would get mad at him for not being enraged at the staff along with me. My heart was so bitter because of my cutting. I would give a tongue-lashing to anybody who would have stood for it. I grew more desperate with each progressive surgery. To date, I have had thirteen facial reconstructive surgeries. Because of the disfigurements that lay hidden beneath their bandages, I know I can count on several more. Destruction caused by my own hand. At this moment, sitting outside with my sweet husband tonight, I feel happy. I sensed a change within me, and the breeze of further changes gently caresses my skin.

The next day, Tim found out that one of his good friends had passed away from a short bout with metastatic cancer that had taken over his brain. We were all relieved that the battle was short, as his suffering was great. Greg and Tim had been friends ever since they were young cub scouts together. They attended all the same schools growing up. Greg was one of the groomsmen at our wedding. I liked him. He was genuine and funny. I remember when I found out he had died. Regret washes over me. Tim and him could have had a much deeper adult friendship if only I had been normal. I didn't want to feel such deep regret ever again.

Greg's funeral service was given by a comical preacher with a thick Irish accent. Greg would have made instant friends with this man. It was a wonderful service that ended with several of his friends and family standing up to tell a humorous or endearing story about Greg. I would still be wiping my eyes from one speech while beginning to laugh at another. I hadn't known he had lived such a full life. It makes me sad that we exist in a world that gives you all the magnificent details that have encompassed a person's life in a pamphlet upon entering the person's funeral. I have discovered so many intricacies about people I have known once they have passed on. As I read the pamphlet with their best photograph strategically placed on the front, I am amazed at the life they led before I met their acquaintance. It is not until they breathe their last that we, as humans, share this pertinent information with each other. What if we began to know the intricacies of a person's life before their breaths have ended? What a different world that would be. But we will remain a stoic society, scrubbing up life's messes with a pseudo-cleaning. We leave the funeral feeling good about ourselves because we actually attended. As if the funeral is the end of the grieving process for the deceased loved one. When in fact, it is merely the beginning.

After the Irish preacher had finished his consoling sermon, we all moved to a fellowship hall for the customary luncheon. I sensed a distinct change in how I was reacting to other people. Instead of merely meeting their eyes with a smile, I started to engage them in conversation. I introduced myself to some of Greg's friends that I didn't know and spoke to each one that I did. Most of them I hadn't seen since our wedding. At the end of it all, as we were walking out the door to leave, an elderly lady with a walker asked me, "What happened to your nose?" My husband, always ready to be my impromptu knight, calmly returns her question with another. "What do you think happened?" This cute elderly lady put her tiny fists in the air, pretending to hit me in the nose. Then she said something about wishing she'd have seen the other guy. She was cute, and she made me laugh. It was a sweet interaction to end our day with.

On the hour drive back to our house, Tim and I talk with each other about Greg. Taking it a step deeper, we began discussing death and dying, being privy to how fleeting all of our lives are. Like the lilies that clothe the grass of the field, which is here today and gone tomorrow. Our lives are expendable and unpredictable. We spend our time gathering and storing up for ourselves, only to be taken while we sleep. Why are we not more like the birds of the air? They neither sow nor reap nor gather into barns, and yet our Heavenly Father feeds them. Are you not of more value than they?

As the summer continued, I found myself taking advantage of every moment that I spent out of bed. I have been diagnosed by my hematologist as "unable to absorb iron". I pleaded with him for some insight. He returned with, "Sometimes, this is just how it is." He was a patient, thoughtful doctor that specializes specifically in disorders of the blood. So I smiled in accordance, but beneath my sweet smile is a flurry of questions that will remain unasked.

It was frustrating for me as I attempted to figure out a specific diagnosis. Spending several hours on the internet, searching my symptoms for matching medical physiology behind the hidden disease that has been destroying my precious time. Making me loathe sleep as it stripped me of feeling fully alive. To no avail, I had such a long list of possibilities, I was more lost than when I had started my investigation. I choked off my endless search and accepted the words of my hematologist. "Sometimes, this is just how it is."

I continued waking up in those darkened, early morning hours. I had learned to enjoy the time I had alone with my thoughts and my newly discovered hobbies. The most important conversations of my day were during this time before the rooster crows. My house is quiet. There is a table lamp behind me, giving off just enough light to let the house know that I am awake. I can still smell the freshly brewed coffee as I sip mine periodically. This is where I find my Lord waiting up for me. It is a great convenience that my God never sleeps because I have needed him at all hours throughout my life. He is as close to me as my very breath. We continue our conversation that began nearly fifty years ago. It has been an ongoing dialogue, with pauses in between. Some pauses lasting much longer than others. Those times I held my back to Him while at the same time complaining that I was in His Shadow. How gracious is our Lord?

This morning I began by asking Him to search my heart and find any darkness hidden within its many crevices and deep caverns. Because He knows my innermost being, He first reminds me. "Stay protected, little one, no one can pluck you from your place as you rest safely in the palm of My Hand." I felt reassured by the words I hear from Him that reverberated within my mind. His Presence calms me. His love embraces my spirit as His peace envelops my body. It makes my soul feel lighter, knowing He is here with me always, even to the end of the age. He is a good, good Father, and I am loved by Him. That's who I am. Once He is certain I am filled to the top with his love and grace, He reminds me of my hidden tools. He is honoring my early morning request as He discloses to me the secrets buried deep within my heart. Nothing is hidden from

His view. My own self-deception keeps these secrets out of sight for me. I am now on a path where He is slowly showing me what is required of me to be healed. As I said before, He is my Counselor. So many people think He is a magic genie. But my Lord does not come with a bottle, but rather a cross. He does not grant me three wishes or wave His magic wand, and Voila', I'm all better. My search for healing and redemption is a journey that will last until it does. He has no boundaries. Not even time can constrain Him. He is probably baffled by how we need to measure our entire life with our inventive concept of time yet waste so much of it. How ironic is that? I decided that I was done performing like a toddler and incessantly asking my Papa, "Why?" Now when I hear His voice, I follow Him without hesitation. I remain seated at our kitchen table as I think about the brutal task I have just been assigned. Although they have not been in use for several months, I still hold possession of them and know of their various hiding places within the walls of our home. "It is time to retire those. They serve no purpose in your life any longer." His words could not have been more clear. It became a day-long, intensely emotional process. Once I thought I had discovered the last hidden tool, I would remember another place to look. During my searches, my mind was pounded with graphic memories of the horrific barbarity I brought upon myself while engaged in hand-to-hand combat, with me as the enemy. It was a bloody time, as I can see now, gathering all of my sharp, puncturing tools that I find splattered with my dry blood, wrapped up in a scarlet-stained tissue. So sick. How could anybody understand? I couldn't understand. But the Lord had placed a fork in my road. "Do you want to understand the why's of life, or do you want to move past them?"

I heard My Shepherd gently whisper His encouraging words of wisdom to me. Seeing these past items of destruction felt overwhelming. My chaotic thoughts landed on a living metaphor. As my hands felt heavy under the weight of the countless crimson tools that they held, it brings to remembrance my tender heart of stone. So many secrets hidden in all its darkened cracks and deep crevices. I knew I was doing better, but the road ahead seems too long. "Sometimes you cannot fix what you have broken." I started with authority and humbleness of heart. "This is too hard, Lord." I fought with Him because of these memories that dominantly haunt my soul. As I stared at all the bloodied instruments that lay before me, horrific scenes flash in my head. Bloody scenes that I have lived through. Too much blood. I began sobbing uncontrollably. The emotions contained within that moment remain unexplainable. I was holding twenty years' worth of tools that I have used to mutilate my face. The dried blood surrounding them had turned to scarlet red from the wetness of my tears, tormenting my inner man. In that glimpse of time, the Holy Spirit that filled my once hollowed soul blazed fire through my veins. I courageously wrapped my past together and threw it in the rubbish. I had this sense of freedom. Something was new. I could feel the change. God is on the move in my life.

# Chapter 10
# Intentionally Left Blank

By mid-summer, my entire family had become keenly aware of a veracious change in me. My husband had retired from his self-appointed assignment as the hawk, hovering over my every move. His time on the job had expired. There was no need to watch over me any longer. Awarding my sweet boy, in the dark flannel shirt, with some well-deserved, necessary sleep. My entire home is filled with this new, welcoming peace. Something that had been missing in our past. We had all gone so long without it; we had forgotten what it feels like. We have trudged through this dark forest for thousands of miles. We have trampled through the brier as its thorns tore at our flesh. Despite standing on the other side with frayed, blood-stained clothes, covered in mud and mire, the warmth of the sunshine feels comforting. Our amnesia is immediately squelched as this new, unimaginable peace courses through our veins.

For the first time in my life, I wasn't pretending any longer. I knew who I was and I had definitely outgrown my plastic mannequin. I felt alive and took every advantage I had to be engaged with people. I discovered that I actually liked most of them. Some of them I have loved all along. I was meeting new people without reservations. I often forgot that I was wearing the bandages until the mirror brought them to light. I consciously made the decision that I was going to be the woman who God created me to be. Scars, bandages, and brokenness too.

If I were outside and spotted a neighbor, we would stop what we were working on and have a friendly conversation with one another. I was not self-conscious of my bandages and scars. Quite the contrary. I had learned to accept my new face. I didn't openly share why I sported facial scars and bandages; my neighbors graciously never questioned it. I found that once I had decided to become my true self while embracing my new face, others also accepted it as a mere fact of life. They did not need to understand the why's in my life. My Spirit within shone through my earthly tent so brightly that my great imperfections were barely visible through the warmth that radiated from the core of my being. The love of my Saviour beamed from within me as I talked endlessly to my neighbor's two sons. Payton is a smarty pants that likes to be tested on the knowledgeable files stored within his intelligent brain. I visited many different websites with trivia questions above his normal academic level and he would virtually answer them all correctly. I was amazed at this young Einstein. He would sit on our front porch with me for hours. After we both grew tired of testing his all-knowing brain, we would begin to talk about his day at school. He was a fifth grader at the same elementary school Isaac had attended. The school was hard for Payton. He was an intelligent, thoughtful boy with a heart of gold. With his twelve years on this

Earth gathering and storing information, he had more wit about him than most adults. Payton never questioned why I looked different from the norm. He didn't care. I once heard a quote that went something like this: "Once you are gone, people will forget what you look like. Rarely, they may remember something you said. But they will never forget how they made you feel." I knew I made Payton feel important and smart and accepted and loved. He, in turn, unknowingly made me feel all those same emotions, minus the smart part. His brother Ridge, one year his junior, would call to me from their basketball hoop. "Watch me!" As I raised my eyes, swoosh! "That was all net, Ridge. Good job!"

From my usual spot on the front porch with his brother, I would enthusiastically holler over to him to catch his attention. Eventually, once he heard the level of accolades he felt he rightly deserved, he would come to join us on the front porch and tell me about his day. Payton and I listened intently to his stories. He had just as many problems with bullies as his brother did, but he didn't give it much attention. "Yeah, they are all just jerks." Although Ridge did not possess the same academic zeal, he had an old soul, just like Payton. They both helped me see it is not what the world feeds me but what I am willing to ingest. If I give it no bother, brushing the idiots of this world off as "all just jerks". Their combustible arrows, once aimed directly at my heart, become extinguished by my indifference. Words that would have normally ruined my day would crash against my tough exterior and fall to the ground long before they could reach my delicate heart.

The Lord has become my everlasting shield, bouncing off the fiery darts from the enemy with His authority over him. He has become my protection and peace in a world filled with neither. Didn't someone once say, "Let the children come to me?" Smart. I enjoyed my conversations with Payton and Ridge immensely. Once it was getting close to the brothers' dinnertime, their mom would come out to gather her two well-fed, hefty, football-playing sons. She and I would talk briefly before they all disappeared behind their front door.

Our next-door neighbor to the north of us have lived in their home for well over a decade now. We have been chummy with them, as our relationship has grown over the years. Dave and Sara, along with their son, Hunter, who happens to be the same age as Isaac. When they first moved into our neighborhood, the boys became fast friends and hung out with each other often. I got to know them pretty well through the boys' friendship, as did Tim. They seemed laid back and would always greet me with a smile. When you live next to somebody for that length of time, you are bound to get to know their ins and outs pretty well. They saw me bandaged often. Sometimes, I would stop by their house to pick up Isaac for dinner, sporting a fresh, unexplained sore on my face.

# FACING IT

Over the years, Sara and I have become good friends. We often visit each other, meeting at our respectable front porches for conversations about anything from our problems to our triumphs and everything in between. I feel closest to her during these special moments of hurting and helping, laughing and giggling, and sometimes downright soul-searching. Several years into our developing relationship, I made the fateful choice to share my deep affliction with her. In just a few words, I was able to explain the history of questions that I knew she had. Who wouldn't? I think I may have shocked her with my admission of self-inflicting all the wounds I bore. I figured she needed a few days to ingest the bombshell I had laid on her lap. I gave her some distance while it exploded in her soul. I didn't want to lose her friendship over the secret my entire life had centered around. And I didn't. If anything, it struck down that great barrier of deception I had formed between us. With my shields down, it allows us to share more secrets with each other, deepening our relationship that much further. Our friendship has only grown sweeter over the years. We talk with each other daily. Often sharing our morning coffee together. Recently, she has told me that she has noticed a definite change in me. I noticed it too. I engaged with her on a more intimate level. Sharing my daily problems as she would share hers. No more lowered face with eyes staring at the ground, attempting to avoid any direct eye contact.

I never wanted to see that look of disgrace in her eyes and I never did. Her husband, Dave, has always called me "Momma". I like the nickname because that is who I am. He has always been kind to me and gives me hugs, even if we see each other at the grocery store. He will stop what he is doing and embrace my five-foot-four larger frame with his six-foot-five slender one. I feel accepted and loved by both of them. Upon writing of their graciousness, I realized I have never told them how much they have enriched my life. They have greatly assisted in my healing by accepting me for who I am and never asking me the dreaded questions about my face. They simply met me where I was without judgment. How beautiful is that? God blessed me with - neighbors that embody grace with gentle, caring hearts and I couldn't be more grateful for them.

Early this August, I noticed some new neighbors moving in next door to the south of us. Once the sun was setting and cooler air filled the evening skies, I walked over to introduce myself, with my husband following shortly behind me. They were wonderful! We all talked and laughed while standing barefoot in our shared lawn space. We knew they were exhausted from moving in, so our introduction was brief. But a seed of friendship had been planted. I didn't avert my gaze and they didn't stare at my bandages. It felt so good to feel human again. To feel worthy of engaging other people. Rather than feeling like the phantom of the opera unable to show my face to anyone.

# FACING IT

About mid-August, we had a blazing outdoor fire in our backyard. All the neighbors came over to enjoy watching the hot dance of the inferno. As we enjoyed the fellowship of good conversation, our new neighbors Aaron and Corrin walked down to join us for the fire. There is something special about sitting around a contained, roaring outdoor fire while reminiscing with friends. Within the darkness, I have found people seem to share more about themselves. The conversation had turned to skydiving, as Dave had just completed his first solo jump and Sara jumped for the first time ever. We were there, watching them and cheering them on as their body came to rest on the ground like a rocket shooting through the grass. It was an exciting adventure for everyone involved. So, Aaron pipes up to tell us of his bungee jumping story. It ends with him in the rebound position, with his belly bouncing back and forth, repeatedly smacking him in the face. "They never tell you about that stuff!" He quipped. "It nearly knocked me out!" Now, everybody's laughter was roaring higher and louder than the crackling fire. Tim placed another log on the smoldering blaze. Our relationship deepened, as did the night.

Summer flew by, as it often does, and it came time to move Isaac into his new apartment in Vermillion. This year's studies required him to relocate and his classes would be resuming in a couple of weeks. A longtime friend of Isaac's came along to help with the heavy stuff. His Uncle Dennis drove a truck up, filled with his bed and couch. Once again, we were blessed with all the help we needed. "Yahweh-Yireh" ... The Lord Provides. Moving the oversized couch to his third-level apartment proved to be the most challenging. They took out a light fixture in the process. The next level up, they crashed into the glass covering of the fire extinguisher. It had previously been broken, with remnants of glass shards filling the carpeting beneath. They moved everything else in with no problems at all. Tim even fixed the broken light fixture. We were on our way to a well-deserved lunch. The boys were all famished. Isaac was excited to be living on his own this next school year. Tim and I were happy for him. Because of his willingness to assist us with the move, Sage and Isaac had also rekindled a friendship from years ago. They visited with one another as they inhaled their lunch. It was as if their song of friendship had not missed a beat. They had the kind of respect and devotion for one another that lasted through the test of time. Allies through life. We all need people like this in our lives. The ones you can depend on when you are in dire need and would be mutually available for them at any time.

We sucked the marrow out of the summer of 2021. Anytime my tired body would allow, we would go on different adventures together. Tim and I visited the Japanese Gardens, which is the ambrosia of parks. You enter under a trellis made of woven, wicker-like wood. Within its boundaries are beautifully manicured bonsai-like trees and a gorgeous pond. The midday sun shines its sparkles on the breathing waters. It has several decorative areas to sit and simply take it all in. We find an empty bench inside a red wooden gazebo for a respite. In the silence, so much is said. As we stand up from our rest, Tim takes hold of my hand. We continue our walk to the end of the path, in which lies the grand finale. I can see the whitecaps of the water as it rushes down the rocky waterfall. Tim and I stand on the bridge, holding hands and I am at peace. Nature has always made me feel close to God.

I am awed at His creations, and now, standing here with my husband, I can feel the presence of my loving Lord God. I cannot resist my child-like prerogative of kicking my bare feet in the coolness of the pond as my sandals lay beside me in the freshly trimmed, green, lush grass. Tim sits next to me with his legs criss crossed. He instantly spots a turtle on a large tree branch sticking out of the water. "See, Elizabeth? Right there." He shows me with his finger pointed in the direction of the turtle's current position. I catch a glimpse of the hard-shelled reptile sunning himself on the log before he slips into the murky waters below.

Savannah and I would often visit the Arboretum with our dog, Shadow. He was a seven-year-old chocolate lab who was a true victor. He had a severe stroke when he was just three years old and it took months to nurse him back to health. He would lay motionless on his bed in our living room as I sat next to him to bring him comfort and tend to his constant needs. We didn't know if he would ever be able to walk again. Despite the facts we observed daily, we held our hopes high for our beloved dog. He eventually began to eat more, gaining strength daily. Until the miraculous day that he got up and took his first few steps. I was overcome by tears of joy. Due to the severity of the stroke, he lost permanent use of his right back leg, to no avail. He was a warrior and nothing could stop him from living his life to the fullest. Smart. He would run with a: step, step, drag, step. This day we brought him out to enjoy the flowers in full bloom and the ample space to run and play. Savannah and I sat on one of their many benches while Shadow sniffed the perimeter of the park's fence, wagging his long tail at all the new scents.

We all attended the Schieffer family reunion in Yankton. A little over an hour's drive from our house. We met at a park on the river and ate fried chicken while reminiscing with one another. They have a reunion every year for Betty and all her twelve siblings. I have continually found it utterly amazing. They are such a big family that would find a way to get together every year without fail. Virtually miraculous in my eyes.

It was during this time of continuous fellowship with my church group, neighbors, family and friends. This uninhibited fellowship brought my spirit back to life. Like the phoenix rising from the ashes. No more pretending. He loves me. And He is more than enough.

# FACING IT

Summer seems to have ended. Maiya left for school with tears in her eyes. We would all miss her. It was her heart and my son's unconditional love that is the most impossible to leave behind. That fresh, new, spring-like love that is true, and present, and deep. My heart broke for them both. I knew I would be seeing them rarely this year. This part of the equation saddens my heart. Albeit, I was happy for them also. They were both following their dreams and they were so committed to those dreams that they were willing to sacrifice the displacement of miles. Never their love. It soon came time for Isaac to leave for the University of South Dakota. It would be nice that he could come home whenever he wanted, being only an hour's drive away. Even though I had that to comfort me, my heart already misses him as I stand in the driveway, waving to him as he pulls away from our house.

Now Tim, Savannah and I make three. The house felt empty once our collegiates had left. It was so quiet. Too quiet. But as time often does, it began to blur the lines of sadness. I was able to see Isaac nearly every weekend because his roommate was an antisocial misfit that I did not care for. Most weekends, Issac would seek refuge at home. A constant in his life, now a place of peace, where he knew he could forever surround himself with those who dearly love him. Love can get a person through the toughest battles. If I could choose only one weapon, that would be it. It could tame a lion's roar as it settles the soul of my son.

I continued my early mornings with My Lord and Saviour. I would spend a portion of my time reading His Word, as the Scriptures would wash over me like a cleansing rain. Every day, I was reassured of who I truly am. Loved by Him. My love grew for Him through time. Together in the stillness of these hours, before the rest of the world had begun its incessant noise and constant chatter, our relationship would deepen. He knows me so well; the very hairs on my head are numbered. Now, I hungered to know Him better. All of the red words glowed with vibrancy in the dimly lit kitchen. Jesus' words, spoken while He took on human form to be present on this earth, came alive and filled my cup until it overflowed. The greatest change of all occurred when the Lord Himself bent down to destroy the chains of shame and guilt in my life. Replacing it with a new hope and a strong sense of who I am within Him. I had become empowered by the new characteristics that defined me. I had been free from my darkened, scarlet-soaked, caustic past for over a year. I have found immaculate freedom in its absence. In the past, whenever I would lock myself behind that bathroom door, my demons would hold me captive as scarlet drops plunged to the floor. Now it is all a distant, yet vivid memory that I have filed in my brain as "Never do again."

I feel compelled to expand on the very idea that I am living out a life in which my urge does not control me. I am no longer plagued by the incessant need to cut my flesh open until I can see the comforting sight of my blood as it drains from my fresh wound. I cannot explain this feeling of freedom. God healed me of my greatest affliction. By His blood, I am saved by grace. I no longer see scarlet stains. I no longer have hiding places. I am no longer frightened that someone may accidentally come upon one of these many spaces and call me out to the floor once again about my disorder. Wanting me to give them answers I did not possess. To this very day, I have no idea what caused me to constantly rip my face apart. My mind has explored immeasurable possibilities. I am not sure I want to know. If God has not revealed it to me, then it is better kept that way. I trust that He knows what is best for me. I am so free. I have made it to the peak and the view from here is breathtaking.

My husband and I have shared thirty years of our lives together, loving one another. We are soulmates and our love for each other remains on fire and unconditional. My children still love our house and have made it their home to this day. My husband says I make the nest too comfortable for them. In the wild, some species of birds begin to add sticks or even thorns in their nests to encourage their children to fly out. He quips with," "You just keep adding more feathers." I like that. I no longer care if I'm the white picket fence mom. Jesus has released me, and I have become a living testimony as I live my life for Him. It makes my heart awaken as I stand tall in the confidence of His love.

At this point, I have also found the gift of letting go of all the past hurts in my life and forgiving those that inflicted my pain. This forgiveness makes my body feel physically lighter. I steadily walk along the path laid before me with ease. Then something would trigger a dark memory. It could be the whiff of a familiar scent in the grocery store as I shop for the week's food for my family. Other times, it was a song whose lyrics could be my testimony. Whatever the trigger, the instant I smelled it, felt it or heard it, images from the recesses of my brain would quickly jump to the forefront of my mind, making it impossible to breathe at times. I remember leaving the grocery store once. A distinct scent brought me back to the awful place that plagued me in my years of my innocence. I left my overflowing grocery cart as I briskly headed for the front door of the building. I lowered my face as I walked through the aisles to my destination. I was embarrassed of my feelings being played out on the stage of life, front and center. Since I began this healing journey, I have abandoned my cold and stoic stature and have come to wear my heart on my sleeve. It didn't matter where I was or who I was with. If I felt it, everybody within a given perimeter around me would know it as they stood in the river of my infinite tears. I ran to the sanctuary of my van, allowing my emotions to fully emit their intensity. I sat, enclosed within the safety of my steel barrier on wheels. Sobbing for half an hour before putting the key in the ignition, revving the engine, and starting for home. These triggers did not occur because of faulty forgiveness. The images playing in my head are there because, at some point in my life, I have lived out the film that contained those gruesome illustrations embedded in my head.

I appealed to my Lord for help through the darkness once again. And once again, He is here for me before my mouth has whispered His precious name. My dark shadows would take flight because of the authority of His name. He would calm my racing thoughts and replace them with His peace that surpasses human understanding. Although I have forgiven my trespassers, it didn't erase what they did to me from my memory. And it most assuredly did not dam the river of tears that followed each one of these caustic memories. I believe that I will never 'get over' my past. It is a part of who I am. But, with the Lord's help, I am getting through it. His Spirit moves within me, making my demons flee. I knew God had a better life in store for me. I have been living out the freedom he eagerly gives me. He is My Papa and He desires the absolute best life has to offer me. Through life's many trials, I have learned that circumstances do not bring me joy. I have enjoyed many circumstances that make me happy. I am talking about true, biblical joy. My life's circumstances will consistently remain askew. I discovered that I could have this undeniable joy way down deep in my soul, notwithstanding my circumstances, through an intimate relationship with Jesus Christ. Loving Him makes me want to be a better person. I long to satisfy My Father with my obedience and faithfulness. He is my purpose for living. After I realized that, everything just seemed to fall into place. Where we all reside is not in our county, or city, or even our own home. We each reside within our own heart, mind and soul. When I gave God control over where I reside, the change within me began to snowball.

The trees are all so beautiful as the autumn breezes find us once again. I love the colors of fall. The vibrant oranges and reds, along with an earth-toned array of light browns and deep purples. Being a South Dakota girl, I wish that autumn would last a while longer. I truly enjoy all the trees, with their vivid array of colors. It seems like the next day, and all those leaves are on the ground and the temperatures have plummeted to below freezing. I believe it is our shortest season. It seems to end just as it has begun. Tim and I took advantage of a couple of these rare autumn days to visit a special place we rediscovered behind the Arboretum. My husband and I gravitate toward the creek that runs through the park. The water level is down, and the creek is shallow and clear. I can see the sand and rocks covering the riverbed's floor. As a child, I loved to find the most distinct rock as a memory of my day. I made this hillside of pebbles, one by one, in the ditch, beside our house. That little girl is alive and well as I wade barefoot into the creek in search of that perfect stone to commemorate spending this precious time with my life-long playmate. My husband has been rearranging the larger rocks forming a small wall where the water streams through, making the noise of a babbling brook. We recorded the tranquil sound of the small stream trickling over the newly arranged rocks. I keep the sound in my iPhone so that I can return to that day by merely pressing play.

We also attended our gargantuan "Downtown Arts Festival". While holding onto each other's hands, we find our way through the crowd of people. I enjoy visiting various booths, each containing a talented designer's finished art pieces. I am particularly amazed at the patience it must have taken to create their unique pieces. It is all mind candy for me, filling my head with so many new ideas to fuel my creativity. Art has become one of my passions. I love creating pictures with pencil or paint. It is simply following the lines. If you change the angle of one distinct line, you can change the look of an entire portrait. I love a quote I recently spotted on Pinterest. "Creative people don't have a mess; they have ideas lying around everywhere." So true. My entire family could attest to that statement.

Throughout the fall season, I continued to receive my infusions to no avail. I would usually wake up at my normal 2 am time, feeling fully refreshed. My creativity flourished in those hours before sunrise. Tim and Savannah would awake around 7 am, as usual, and we would all have coffee together until they both had to go to their respective places to begin work, around eight. Savannah was fortunate to have a much shorter commute. I normally would stay awake a couple more hours before retiring to my bed. I would sleep for quite a while, then never felt the best for the rest of the day. My body ached, as did my head. It felt like a serious case of the 'blahs' nearly every day. I wore my slouched composure around the house for a short status update before returning to the sanctity of my bed once again. I could go all week with my only human contact being the one hour I had with Tim and Savannah each morning. It could have been depressing, being alone for 23 of my 24-hour day. Day after day. But I did not wish to fall down that chasm again. There were too many assets on the line.

I needed to prevent that demon of depression from deafening me with his thunderous boom. With each thought of sadness or self-pity, I would replace it with a comforting chunk of Scripture. And the peace of God, which transcends understanding, guarded my heart and my mind in Christ Jesus. Whatever is true, whatever is noble, whatever is right, whatever is pure, whatever is lovely, whatever is admirable…if anything is excellent or praiseworthy, I thought about such things. God saved my mind from succumbing to this demon of depression that has seen its inferno encompass me in the past. As those familiar fiery darts of the enemy try to fuel my depression, the Lord rains down peace and joy in my mind, heart and soul. Trusting God is a choice. One I must continually make.

I have previously written about my deep love of song. So, as

# FACING IT

Tim and I were out running errands one day, we closely listened as the radio spoke of a concert. For King and Country were coming to Sioux Falls for a Christmas Concert in less than two weeks. Their music spoke directly to my heart. I would find myself sitting on our front porch, headphones in place, as their harmonious voices sang to my soul. I invariably began crying. I listened to their music with that deep down, genuine joy in my heart. We sit in the cheap seats at the concert, but when the Spirit of the Lord is present, this entire world cannot contain Him. It is hard to believe that this is the first concert ticket I have ever purchased. I stood in the back row with my hands raised in praise of my gracious God. My worship of the Lord has changed so much, as His love has transformed my spirit. In the past, I felt like I should have my spirit contained in this unopened, plain brown, unremarkable box. Unable to dance undignified, as David did, in his fire for the Lord. I felt I had to restrain my body because of what others might think. Then I had an epiphany during a song at church one morning. I am not here to bow down to the constraints that society strictly applies to us. I am here solely to show God how much I love him by worshiping Him with my mind, my soul, and my body. So that's exactly what I did at this very special concert. In some songs, I would sway back and forth as I mouthed each word of the lyrics.

In other songs, I was still, with my arms raised, sobbing, overcome by the truths of what my Savior has done for me. Being fully God and fully human, He was also completely aware of what His death and resurrection held within it. All the suffering he would have to endure on His journey to the cross. He also knows the end. Living together with Him in a paradise that He created. My tears turned to that of overflowing joy. I feel His presence, as close as the breath still contained within my lungs. The entire experience was like a revival of my spirit. And on that cold winter night, I felt the fresh spring rains in the soil of my soul.

I still wear my 'Priceless' pendant often. During one of my early morning creativity sessions, I strung a strand of muted pink and turquoise seed beads as a necklace for it. The first time I listened to the song "Priceless", it played so loudly in my ears that I could barely hear it. But I felt it. Each and every word piercing through my soul…tears stream down the sides of my eyes and leave a salty taste in my mouth. This is one of those songs that I feel the lyrics as my testimony. "For the lonely, and the ashamed, the misunderstood and the ones to blame. But if we could start over, we could start over; we could start over. For God only knows what you've been through. God only knows what they say about you. But there's a kind of love that God only knows."

That Christmas was filled with joy. For the first time ever, each of us participated in decorating the tree. We were all engaged with one another. A piece of exceptional wit would be spoken and we would all crack up in laughter. I don't think the rest of my family realizes just how much our lives have changed. Being the one whose life has been transforming, I was keenly aware of the newfound happiness in my family's interactions, inspired by the stress-free zone my metamorphosis had created. That Christmas Eve, as we all open our presents, we truly enjoy each other's company. My thoughts are of the night of my Savior's birth and how grateful I am that He lives.

As we change out last year's calendar for the present year of 2022, COVID's roar has been greatly diminished as restrictions are lifted and we are all able to be in public without masks once again. I was glad that the virus had taken a respite from our nation. The constant hand washing and sanitizing would make Tim's hands raw. I am so very blessed to have a husband that does not mind being the sole breadwinner. I know his biggest concern is my well-being. I feel constantly embraced by his love, whether he is with me or not. Savannah continues working from home for Avera Healthcare. However, I can sense her restlessness for something better in life. An occupation that makes her wake up feeling enthused because she has a career she loves. Maiya and Isaac have just left to return to the spring semester at their Universities that span four hours apart. They keep in constant communication, talking daily about their assignments and accomplishments. Even with the distance, their love remains strong. I am so happy that they found each other.

The beginning of the new year feels like the dawning of a

whole new life for me. I have developed an intimate relationship with God, the Spirit and Jesus in one. I am filled with the Holy Spirit and am sowing seeds whenever and wherever I can see barren land in people's souls. I continue receiving my infusions and my physical health has not wavered. Although my outer man is wasting away, my inner man is being renewed, day by day. The Lord has been so, so good to me. I am filled with humility in His awesome presence.

My early mornings with my Lord continue with great fever as I ask Him to search me and know my heart. I plead with him to test me for my anxious thoughts and to lead me to life everlasting. As I pray with the words of Psalm 139 running through my head, My Lord answers me through the quiet stillness. "Someone is on your list that you still haven't forgiven." I knew what He was asking of me and it seemed an impossible task. But I serve the God of impossibilities, as I have come to personally discover for myself throughout this long journey He and I are on. My hand reaches for the list of names I have tucked in the back of my bible. I already know who He is speaking of. "She has tortured me for so many years, though, Lord. How will I ever forgive her?" My eyes scan the coffee-stained piece of scratch paper in front of me. I scroll down the list, seeing each name that I have previously crossed off. One at a time, as my forgiveness overcame their offenses, I became free from the chains that bound them to me. I quickly spot the last remaining name on the list. The only one that hasn't been scratched out with my pen until it was illegible. No, this name stood out like it was written in bold text. It simply read, "me". "How could I ever forgive someone who has brought my family such great pain? For decades I brought turmoil to their lives. How Lord?" True to form, I have chosen my most grueling task for last. The gift of forgiveness for how burdensome I have been to my family. I have punished them without cause, generating grave fear and confusion with no relief. For twenty years of my life, I wandered through the same dark forest, like a wearisome labyrinth. It exhausted everyone involved in this perplexing, titanic-sized maze. But I felt compelled to be obedient to My Lord, as He has remained so faithful to me. I said a simple prayer of forgiveness. When I came to the part of my prayer when I spoke the trespasses out loud, I paused. I hesitated as my body trembled and my hands clasped in front of my face became wet with my tears. My mind could not find the right words to explain to the Lord all I have done that made everything go wrong. I sheepishly asked God to "forgive me for cutting my face and making my family suffer. Through the authority of the precious name of Jesus Christ, my Lord and my Savior, Amen." I went through the same motions of forgiveness that I had with the other names on my list, but I felt much different this time. Instead of feeling lighter, I felt the world's weight on my shoulders, remembering the torment caused by my offenses. The question still lingers in my head, "Why?" Although I had several hypotheses, none of them seemed like any type of answer that I had assiduously been searching for. But, when I ask my brain a question, it is hard-wired to search until it finds an answer. My mind was bellowing every possible cause, cutting and bruising my core being with every exploiting explanation. "It's because you are a loser. You do not deserve the freedom you carry today. Do you forget all the lives you have disturbed? Go, now. Look at what you've done to your face. You are a raging psychopath. That is why you single-handedly destroyed your face." My consciousness refused to accept any of these caustic suggestions as my new theory. It also would not accept forgiveness from my Lord. After all the willing suffering on His path to Golgotha, I feel sad and guilty. My sins do not deserve the grace of my Lord. I can forgive the rest, but my sins, I will carry around in my back pocket. Always present to remind me of who I was. I alone participated in these unforgivable sins, leaving chaos and destruction in my path. I blamed myself for all the cares of the world because of my great shame.

It was a bitterly cold winter. Too cold to snow. We've only had three severe blizzards. Each causing blowing snow with such high winds that visibility was nil. Snow drifts gather outside our exterior doors. From our large picture window, I watch Tim clear the sidewalks, dressed in his full cold-weather get-up, topped with a heavy, warm wool stocking hat. I sip my coffee from the warmth of our home. I feel so blessed. The Lord has given me much. A husband that says, "He's addicted to me." A son and a daughter that loves me dearly and whom I love too much, as my heart nearly bursts from the surplus contained within its walls. The extreme weight of unforgiveness feels much lighter, but I have not allowed it to be released completely. Throughout the winter months, I have struggled with this problematic forgiveness of self. I am in the process of acknowledging the hurt. The constant stream of unforgiveness coursing through my veins, with only myself to blame for my prolonged season of shame. The devil tries to trick me by whispering in my ear. "You are not good enough to call yourself a Christian. You are too messed up. Too broken. I try to fight him, but my mind continued searching for the true reason behind my twenty-year psychosis. I felt the need to reserve the right to punish myself for my grave iniquity instead of surrendering that right to the Lord.

In the first week of February, our loving warrior of a dog took on quite a spell. I am unsure of why he slipped away so quickly, but he did. One day, he was going on a long walk with his step, step, drag, step pattern. He thoroughly enjoyed sniffing every tree, weed and bush his sense of smell led him to. The next day, I noticed a harsh cough coming from deep within his throat. I immediately made an appointment with our veterinarian. Sitting in the waiting room, he acted just like his normal self. Pulling at the leash with such great strength, I could not hold him back from encountering his newly found furry friend. The vet prescribed some antibiotics and steroids for his bad cough. I left feeling encouraged, with high hopes that this medicine would make Shadow feel better. The following morning, instead of seeing him sprawled out in his extra-large dog bed, I could hear him whining from the foyer. He couldn't move and whimpered if I stopped petting him. So I sat with him until the sweet visiting veterinarian arrived. She sits down by Shadow as she introduces herself to all of us. She gently makes a dough-like impression of his paw as a remembrance for us to hold onto. Her hands are compassionate as she injects him with a deep sedative. His tongue is hanging out of his mouth. I place my hand on his chest to feel for the rise and fall of a breath. It is there. We all cry as we say our final goodbyes. My vision was altered by the eruption of tears. Finally, she injects him with a liquid that instantly makes his heart stop. My hand placed on his chest now remains still. He is gone. I think he will be with us in heaven. My heart is broken over losing Shadow. Our home feels empty without him in it. In attempts to console us, our neighbors started to bring Gio, their Bully dog over for cuddles and kisses. Each morning, without fail, Sara would drop him off at our front door around seven and we would bring him home around five. Nice set-up. It was like a doggie daycare for Gio. He loves all the attention and it is therapeutically healing us. He brings tranquility to our home as he softens the extreme blow of our grief. A couple of weeks into this gift of solace, Gio had learned the pattern and started shooting straightaway for our front door first thing every morning. He has high-tailed it over as early as 5 am. But I am awake, so I love it. I love seeing his squished up face and folded ears. I adore seeing him looking for me through the thin window panel on the side of our front door. Once he catches sight of me, he wags his tail so hard his little butt wiggles. He makes me smile. It's those small joys in life that sometimes get overlooked. The things that are so obviously advantageous, I am learning to embrace these small joys that take hold of my heart.

It wasn't long before I noticed the lilac tree beside our house blooming tiny violet buds that spread across each branch. I enjoy watching God's creations come to life before my very eyes. Small shoots that will become bright yellow daylilies are sprouting through the hardened ground. We are getting a welcomed increase in the amount of light every day as the night's darkness is diminishing. Soon, I spotted my first monarch butterfly, as a blur of orange and black fluttered by me.

I continue my early morning talk sessions with the Lord as He asks me to dig deeper into my relationship with Him. I envision him fully tattooed with all the sins of my past. Lost and without purpose. I tortured my family for twenty years, leaving me with layers of shame and guilt. Inconsequential. Useless. No good. Dirty. Broken. Yet, I see Him, with outstretched hand, inviting me to "Follow Him". He appeals to me for true, absolute forgiveness of my arch nemesis. The one who resides within this tent the world sees. I know the fault of my burdens. I can see the misery, torment and disgrace I have caused others. However, I have been walking much lighter these days, as most of my baggage has been eternally dropped off along this path the Lord and I are on. It has been refreshing for my dry bones. God brought them back to life when He healed me. Our relationship has become so real. So intimate. much, the level of intimacy that brings true joy and peace and love. It is an eternal flame. Albeit, I can feel that there is a higher level of freedom that I am missing out on because of my strong aversion to forgive myself. The last one on the list. This Sunday morning, while up in the darkest hours, spending time with my Lord, I pray for divine strength, healing and freedom while trying to appease His last request.

During our morning service at church, Pastor Mike began his sermon with a simple story, as he often does. A metaphor pertaining to the topic at hand. Today, he gave us a history lesson on what has become known as "The Pioneer Trail." I am no history buff, so I hope I remember his story correctly. There was a trail, amidst the 1800s, that people struggled down with their fully loaded, horse-drawn wagons from the Midwest to the West Coast. Most of those families' destinations were either Oregon or California. It was a grueling journey and nearly every family who completed the trip had lost a loved one along the way due to disease or injury.

Everyone who traveled this well-known trail made the same

mistake. Each family on this long, backbreaking path had packed way too much stuff. All throughout the initial several miles, people had left behind stoves, pianos, furniture and a large amount of baggage. It was slowing them down and making this formidable trail even more intimidating to manipulate. Each of the families who made it to their final destination had dumped a good portion, if not all, of their baggage, making them travel with haste as the dusty, bumpy, old trail would grumble under the wooden wagon wheels. At this point in the sermon, I am fairly sure where our fearless pastor is taking us with this true-to-life story. He referenced bible verses from the prophetic book of Isaiah. "He was pierced for our transgressions."

He also referred to Second Corinthians. "The devil is good at deceiving us. He is quick to give us excuses." As the preacher's sermon spoke those last few words, it stung my spirit. How many excuses have I pleaded before the Lord? Reasons that I should not be forgiven. My sins are too great. I hurt too many innocent bystanders. So many years lost. The pastor told truths of how the Lord has laid on Him the iniquity of all of us. "Could I be included in that 'all' reference?" My thoughts wondered if this vagabond could be worthy of such a sacrificial gift. Pastor Mike then plays this video clip that begins with a rugged man just getting out of bed. His skin is flawless, with no ink covering any portion of it. He has thick, dark brown hair and a full beard. He is wearing a plain white shirt, black jeans and flip-flops. He enters the basement of this old, brick building, which is obviously his tattoo parlor. He sits down on his adjustable stool, and almost immediately, his first customer comes down the stairs and slides into his special, black leather chair.

The customer has a concerned look on his face and as he turns his wrist, he has a tattoo that reads, 'depressed.' The bearded man with the ink turns the word into 'confident'. Many more people enter this burly man's tattoo shop. They all take a seat and humbly show him their tattoo with a look of desperation in their eyes. He takes one look, picks up his ink pen and goes to work. He must continually move his long, black hair behind his ear, enabling him to see what he is working on. One young man shows him his bicep, encircled with the word, 'Fear', and he transforms the old ink to read 'Trust.' An older man enters the shop and slips into this master's chair. He has visible dirt on his face and his clothing is disheveled. He makes eye contact with the tattoo artist as he hesitantly rolls up his sleeve, revealing the word, 'Useless.' Once again, the shop owner grabs his ink pen and changes this man's tattoo to read, 'Purpose.' The man's eyes light up as a smile appears on his face.

A young woman ventures inside to take a seat in this miraculous tattoo shop. She pulls up her sleeve to reveal the word, 'Addiction', which is promptly replaced with 'Affection'. She looks down at her new ink and gives the man a look of joy before leaving. The last customer of the day is a young boy, about 16 years of age.

# FACING IT

It is difficult for him to navigate the entrance, as he struggles with his forearm crutches, virtually dragging his feet behind him as he walks. He pulls down the front of his shirt, revealing his tattoo, which boldly reads, 'OUTCAST', and covers the entirety of his chest. This one brings great stress to the tattoo artist and as he wipes the sweat from his brow, I can sense his exhaustion. He patiently works on the deep, dark ink. This young boy takes much longer than any of his other customers. Finally, the tattoo artist sits back to reveal the restored ink that reads, 'ACCEPTED'.

He looks at the store keeper with a smile of pure joy as he struggles to walk away. He transformed each one of them into something life-giving. He sighs heavily as he rises from his stool. We see him turn around, revealing the tension in his back. He seems weary. It is then that he lifts his shirt off, revealing all the tattoos he has ever removed, inked permanently on his back, arms, sides and chest. Thief, liar, guilt, shame, self-righteous, despair, anger, wasted, greed, invisible, addicted, depressed, jealous…He is covered in ink. My ink. He is pierced for my transgressions. Once again, I'm a sobbing mess of a pitiful human being. I thought to myself, "If I was the first one to take a seat in this special tattoo parlor, he would not have any room left on his body to take on another customer. My sins would cover him from head to toe. My heart breaks for Jesus. I nailed him to that tree. My hand embraces the handle of the hammer as I pound the nails into my innocent

Savior. Pastor Mike ended his sermon with Romans 3:23…for all have sinned and fall short of the Glory of God. He ended with a short prayer and within that final prayer, he let silence overtake his spoken word. He had instructed us to use this time to get right with the Lord.

I turned, rested my elbows on my knees, covering my face with my hands, and cried out to My Savior, "Please, Lord. Forgive me for hurting myself for twenty years of my life. I feel so guilty, knowing all the missed opportunities, because I held back, too embarrassed and ashamed to be seen. I have held my entire family captive with darkness. Forgive me for all my iniquities. I love you, Lord. I want to do what pleases you. I desperately want to be made whole. Please take this rugged, old baggage. It is so heavy and cumbersome. I have been carrying it with me for so long. I give you control, Lord. I do not wish to punish myself for my sins any longer. I surrender it to You. Thank You for walking beside me on this lifelong journey. Please award me with Your divine strength, healing and freedom. In the Authority of the Precious Name of My Lord and Savior, Jesus Christ. Amen."

I truly meant it this time. I wasn't just repeating the same forgiveness prayer like I had been. Day after day, so many times, that it is starting to sound more like a chant. This was a pure, desperate cry for help from My Lord. With my power willingly released to Him, He made me anew. My heaviest piece of baggage is finally gone. I feel fully human. Instead of "shame" and "guilt",

He has inked "strong" and "courageous" on my skin. Instead of being an outcast, I am now an overcomer and a warrior. The last links of the chain are broken. I can feel His bright light fill the once-darkened cavern in my heart. The past can no longer hold me back. I am Free, in the precious name of Jesus!!! I am free indeed!

# Chapter 11
# Traveling Light

Yes, I realize that chapter ten is missing. It is a chapter that, although written, will remain untitled and untold. It is a story that only God and I are privy to. I have prayed through this decision and my answer was clear. It is a part of my journey that would hurt too many people. Therefore, it will continue to remain between me and God. Actually, I thought my story had ended at the end of chapter nine. But it most definitely had not. I am now living out the chapters of this book as I am writing it. I will explain to you why there is no chapter ten. But it takes me a while to get to that point. So hang in there.

At the end of chapter nine, I vividly told of the freedom I felt when I forgave myself. The last person on the list. It was magnificent. I was embodied by God's grace. My chains were broken. I felt it. The distinct end of my story. But as the saying goes, 'If you want to make God laugh, tell Him your plans'. I'm sure God is smiling down on me now.

In mid-April, my husband had heard on the radio about MercyMe coming to Sioux Falls. One of my all-time favorite bands. A definite must-see. I snatched up some cheap seats before they were all gone. I admire Bart's story and the guts it took him to make it into a movie. My soul is refreshed in each of the bands' songs and

I could probably sing each word of their lyrics. I was so happy when the concert venue opened and I had an enormous amount of energy. I think my adrenaline played a part in how alert I was that night. The Holy Spirit illuminated radiantly inside of me as each song was played. Partway through the concert, they changed the backdrop to a campfire setting. Each one of the band members sitting back, relaxing, as the true-to-life campfire warms their bodies. I remember Bart saying that he had regretted wearing his long-sleeved sweatshirt. Their cheeks were all a little pink from the heat.

Robby's seat doubled as his instrument. It was a cajon, which is basically a box drum. It has a different sound. Like when some musicians use chains on drums to give that new spectacular echo. I liked how it was so simple yet resonated pleasantly through my ears with each tap on its sides. Bart told us all the story of the campfire. It is where they go when a full day's work is done. It is their place of rest and fellowship. This was when the concert became deeper for me. It's like the first half was to make you want to stand up and worship music and the second half was the 'let's get real' part. Once again, music has affected my life in such a meaningful way. This concert, now in the Spring, floods my soul with its living waters.

The concert, being on the 28th of April, practically brought us into the beautiful month of May. One of my favorite months. The weather is perfect for me, with lows ranging in the 50s and the high temperature rarely over 70 degrees. The bugs are still in their hibernation, so no need for the fly swatter or Bug-a-salt this time of year. I sit outside on our redwood patio. My husband has just painstakingly finished sanding and staining each grain of wood that the twenty-year-old set contains. I have said it before, and it is worth repeating: we do not give up on people or things in this family. If my husband had a choice between spending $20 to fix an old, nostalgic bird feeder, or $10 for a new one, you would find him at home with a screwdriver, hammer, clamps and wood glue, missing twenty dollars from his wallet.

Whatever it takes to bring our birdhouse back to life, providing sustenance for my sparrows that bring me fresh songs each new morning. The sunshine dances on my face as it sparkles through the frolicking leaves overhead. I close my eyes and spend time enjoying its warmth and light. One important truth I have learned throughout this journey is to take my time with life. Walking down my path with patience so that I may receive joy from the little things that I may have previously overlooked. Moments I have been too consumed with my own thoughts to stop and notice the beauty of life. However, at this exact moment in time, I am receiving joy from the warmth on my face, as I can still see the dancing light, even with my eyes closed. The outdoors brings me great comfort and delight. God's creation. It is so very intricate and amazing. I am blessed to have this brilliant day that has been gifted to me. I am thankful and my heart pours out its gratitude to anyone that may come across my path.

One fine Spring day, I drove to the clinic close to our home to get my blood drawn for extensive testing. The next day, I received a call from my hematologist's office. My iron levels had once again plummeted. I am not at all surprised by this. It has been an ongoing affliction in my life. Labs, infusions, labs, infusions, repeat. Although I dislike the process, I know these infusions are the only reason I am able to get out of bed each morning. The nurse notified me that my doctor had chosen a completely different infusion for me this time and an appointment was set up for the following morning. They called my name and the nurse brought me back to one of the all too familiar, dingy-colored, pleather infusion recliners. She placed my IV with ease as her confident hand slid the needle directly into my antecubital vein, leaving the cannula in its place for the healing liquid to flow through my veins. Then she hung the heavy, clear plastic bag filled with brown liquid, which has become my energy source. I was thankful it gave me time to enjoy this new life. Free of those rusty, old chains that held me back for so long. My heart overflows with love and compassion for my fellow human being. After several hours and two bathroom breaks, my brown liquid concoction had completely emptied itself through my veins in hopes that it will give my energy level a boost. I thanked the nurse and promptly left. I dislike sitting there for so many hours, connected to a bag on a long pole, with nothing to do, but blast my music in my eardrums to drown out the noises of the hospital and try, most futilely, to fall asleep.

Each day, we were blessed with more light. Unfortunately, this extra light brings extra heat along with it. I have become intolerable of high temperatures. If I have to be outside on a hot and humid day, you will find me under the nearest shade tree. Although each morning, waking up around two am, the temperature is more than tolerable. It is perfect. The bugs are all asleep, minus the moths, but they bring me no bother. I continue to enjoy this time I have with the Lord. I would thank Him for my many blessings and ask for His redemption once again. This time, however, it was not for my redemption. I am redeemed and who the Son sets free shall be free indeed! Instead, it was an intercessory prayer for other loved ones that do not revel in His saving grace. I kept praying for other people, all the while ignoring this gnawing sensation from deep within my soul. I knew why it was there. I was hoping if I ignored it long enough, it would work itself out and I would be free again. Does that ever work? That pseudo logic surely wouldn't fix my vehicle's engine, nevertheless, I have been depending on it to fix my very soul. I can be exceptionally hard-headed at times.

This morning was different. I could feel my anger and rage welling up inside of my bones with great ferocity. The darkness has been unbound from its deeply-rooted, hollow crypt in the viscera of my heart. I can feel it pumping through my arteries and filling my body with an emotion that I can distinctly, physically detect within my bones. I experienced this ominous, murky, gut-wrenching feeling that I knew could be ignored no longer. It was time for chapter 10. I was exhausted from running away from it. I turned, and my Savior was already there, sitting next to me. He met me this morning with his softest of whispers. I place my hesitant hand in His, and I could sense His strength, filling me with the fortitude to complete this harrowing act. There was a name I had previously crossed off the list of people that required my forgiveness. When I initially forgave this person, I did seem lighter, just like I had with the others. I'm not certain if I hadn't fully forgiven them or if I had traveled backward on my path, enabling me to pick up the baggage I had once set down.

Either way, it was time to pick up that piece of loathsome luggage and open it. Indeed. I needed to face it. My thoughts whirled inside my head. Every sin committed against me came to the forefront of my mind. I could feel my hands tremble as I genuinely felt the pain I had endured. The memories still haunt me, and in this present moment, I can feel the heaviness of it all. I am allowing this lone person to keep me in bondage. My spirit is filled with fear and anxiety. As I continue digging deeper into the issue at hand, I can feel the darkness, once again, coursing through my blood. I carefully open up the threadbare, oversized baggage. It is filled with evil and misdeeds. It contained every crime committed against my body and each immoral act that left me with feelings of shame. For each and every injustice, I surrendered my right to punishment. I took the last of the pains contained within this baggage, along with my feelings of righteous anger, and placed them all at the feet of Jesus. He released the barriers of the crypt, allowing His light to fill the darkness that had been residing there. My spirit, which once screamed in agony, is now screaming with genuine victory. I am overcome by His grace and provision in my life. The pages of this book are coming to an end, but my life with Him is eternal. 'I am unsure of where You are taking me next, Lord. Lead the way, and I will follow You.'

# Epilogue

"And one day she discovered that she was fierce and strong and full of fire and that not even she could hold herself back, because her passion burned brighter than her fears."

-Author unknown-

I believe this quote was written for me at this exact time in my life. It embodies how I feel and the genuine way I portray myself to the world. It is currently 2:38 am. I have made freshly brewed coffee, which I am currently enjoying. I sip its sweet, warm nectar through my straw. I am thankful for this dark blanket that covers our sky, with its only illumination from the crescent-shaped moon and infinite stars. I am thankful that God saved my life on that fateful day in August. Time has distanced me from this miraculous day in history for over six years now. It feels like a lifetime ago. I have traveled through so many different lives. My life with Tim, with my plastic mannequin in place, until she wasn't. I futilely struggled to find six feet under as my memories and self-mutilating disorder plagued me to the very core of my being. Dragging me, along with my entire family, down an obscure back alley that nobody knew how to traverse.

Sitting here now, on my second pot of coffee, I am living in the light. Without secrets. Free of the shame and guilt that once tortured my mind with its repetitive demeaning thoughts. My Lord has met me here this morning, as he has each morning, to help me write down these stories that summarize my life. During the darker portions of my writings, my body would suffer from headaches, as well as body aches and extreme lethargy. I am an empathic person, so when I feel a strong emotion, it's like I am in the ocean as the tide is coming in. I just stand there, letting each big wave knock me down, as it fills my lungs with splashes of water, making me cough incessantly. I hurry to stand up as the next wave comes crashing in, and I repeat the process all over again. Sounds pretty exhausting, right? That is how deep emotions are for me. I wait for them to knock me down, just to get back up again and find they are still present in my soul as the waves knock me down once again, making me choke on the water from its forceful impact that I was not prepared for. Writing this has not been easy, but in life, I find the toughest battles end with the sweetest victories. And I can honestly say that I am victorious. As I write to you this early morning, I have a cute little Ewok tucked inside my shirt pocket. My husband slipped it into bed with me yesterday as I lay sleeping, exhausted from finishing my book. I slept for three straight days after the last word had been typed. Tim has been continually checking on me, and yesterday evening, I noticed my special furry stuffed friend tucked beside me in bed. My husband is such a sweet-hearted man. He knows how much I like Ewoks. I can distinctly recall when the movie, "Return of the Jedi" was released. I was nine years old.

# FACING IT

Mike and I traveled all the way from Mitchell to Sioux Falls to see it the day it was released. May 25th, 1983. I felt so important to be traveling an hour's drive away with my big brother. To see this amazing new movie that he talked about non-stop for the entire drive from our house to the movie theater. Watching the show through nine-year-old eyes, I hated Jabba the Hutt and fell in love with the high-pitched, furry, witty Ewoks. I wanted one of my own. Now, this morning, I finally have one. Being present is so important. Even while I was sleeping, my husband was present for me. He compassionately lay that stuffed animal beside me in the bed, quietly, so as not to wake me. It's as if we were both nine years old again. That's how life is sometimes. That little boy or girl comes out in us in the most peculiar ways. Through my experiences, she has come out to clean herself from the dirt splattered on her by those who were supposed to love her. But these days, she visits me when I am at the brook with my husband in search of my perfect rock to take home with me, memorializing our time spent together. I only let that little girl out to play when in the trusted companionship of my husband. Who is legitimately "addicted to me."

It is September 22, 2022, and it is currently 46 degrees outside. Our first full day of autumn. It practically freezes before the trees have begun to change their color from vibrant green into blazing orange and red. I know I complain about how short this season is each and every time the end of September is here. It is no surprise, as it has continued to be our shortest season since we became a state in the late 1800s. I am sitting at my laptop, which has become my confidant, sharing secrets that it holds within its storage. Although my last laboratory tests proved that my body contained half the amount of iron the normal person would have, my hematologist has decided to forego this infusion, awaiting the results from my next lab draw, which is scheduled one month out. Throughout the time it has taken me to record this story of my life, I have found energy from my Spirit, as my journey has been lightened from all the baggage I once held so dear. There is a phenomenon that occurs when recording memories that haunt me. It is as if when they are clear to me in black and white, they are released from the confines of my brain, making them easier to deal with in the light. It helps me process the shame and guilt that once filled my bones and fueled my life. God works in mysterious ways. It is hard to phanthem how, in this big world filled with over eight billion people, I am able to have such an intricate relationship with Him. Why would He choose to consistently show up in my life? I suppose that is the definition of omnipresent. I am left with more questions than answers when I try to comprehend it all. My God, and my Lord and Savior, Jesus Christ, who knew His destiny before breathing His life into the dust, creating Adam. He knew I would be sitting here in this early morning darkness while the rest of my family is asleep, writing this epilogue as the finale of my autobiography. He is all knowing. He is privy to information that the future year holds within my life. Time is without limits for our awesome God. Yet he gives it to us in tiny slices because He will never give us more than we can bear.

It is now 6:32 am. I have been awake for over four hours. I have been spending my quiet time with the Lord. I find it is easier to hear His whispers in the silence these early mornings carry with them.

We all reside comfortably together: My husband and I, my daughter, with her home office right next to her bedroom upstairs, and my son and his girlfriend, in their downstairs hideaway. I have remained sober from the time I released its power over me. From my soul to God's hand. I was freed from its grasp and have abstained for two years now.

7 am: Tim and Savannah wake up as expected. We have coffee and talk about a dream that Savannah had last night and the song that was in Tim's head as he was waking up. Our normal, routine morning conversation. Then it is time for our joint bible study. Virtually every morning, without fail, we read from scripture and take notes on what we have read. When everyone has made their last notation, we discuss what we have just read and any insights we may have had. It is such an awesome thing to be a part of. My soil is tilled, the seeds have been planted and I am a beautiful, fruitful

tree.

Our neighbor, Sara, comes in for coffee as Gio has led her over to our front door, waiting to be let in from Sara's gentle knock. Yes, this wonderful Bully has continued his routine. We have decided not to get a dog yet, as Gio has become our part-time dog. All of the benefits, without any of the liability. But I love him, so I still feel responsible for him. He has benefited our entire family with his sloppy kisses and soft fur, begging to be pet.

It is now 8:12 am and everyone has left me, minus Gio. He has sat beside me on his special rug throughout most of this book-writing journey that life has granted me. Alexa is playing Christian radio in the background. "Masterpiece" by Danny Gokey. I know it by heart.

Being awake for nearly seven hours and my eyelids are beginning to feel heavier than usual. I make myself a sandwich, and Gio and I hit the rack. After a couple of hours of restful slumber, we are up and ready to go outside. It is a beautiful day. The chilly early morning temperatures have risen as the sun fills the air with its 67-degree heat. Perfect. I sit on my front porch, enjoying the sunshine. I hear my birds singing to one another as they perch around the perimeter of our birdbath, filled with fresh water. Once Gio trots back to our front door, I know it is time to go back inside. He is such a little tank. He is short and stout and his face is all wrinkled up and he snorts when he breathes. Absolutely adorable. I am blessed to have him as my daily companion.

I am going to take this opportunity to tell you more about my current living conditions. My nose and upper lip remain greatly disfigured under my bandages. Because of my constant low blood iron, I have not even called my plastic surgeon. She has been my doctor through each and every surgery and I am aware that she will refuse me as a surgical candidate until I can stabilize my lab values. I feel like I let her down each time I go into her office with a new self-inflicted injury. And each time, she patches my face with skin grafts. Now I must return to her again, with not one, but two, grave defacements. I am glad for the pause between my surgeries this time. Because I know I am free from the chains of my intense urges to cut my face open. The Great Physician has healed my mind. I see my Psychiatrist every three months. He is a wonderfully patient man. On one of my first visits with him, he instructed me on the importance of seeing a counselor. I'm sure it helped, but I hated it. I dislike telling someone my darkest thoughts, and then when my 50 minutes are through, my session is over. "What the hell am I supposed to do with all these parts of my psyche that have spilled over our discussion and onto your floor?" I desperately wanted to ask my psychologist each time our visit had abruptly ended for her next client. Because of this, the dark thoughts followed me out the door of the clinic to be enclosed with me inside the safety of my vehicle. I put the keys in the ignition, hoping to make it out of the parking lot. But before I could turn the key, my dark thoughts turned to darker emotions as a flood of tears broke through their dam. Once I could calm myself, I would drive fifteen minutes to our home, sobbing all the way.

The session left an ominous cloud above my head for the rest of that entire day. Sometimes, I suppose, dry bones should not be brought back to life. After performing this unhealthy ritual for a full year, I talked to my psychiatrist about it, and he said that I could stop and just see him alone. He likes me. He has been my psychiatrist for over five years now. It is their office policy to see a psychiatrist, you must also be under the weekly care of one of their psychologists. My doctor likes to follow the rules. Yet he breaks them for me. His compassion is so apparent, making it nearly visible to the naked eye.

Tim, our constant and our rock, is past his thirty-year mark at Fred the Fixer. He works so hard for us. I am grateful for this sweet, cute boy in the dark, flannel shirt. Savannah has begun to take classes online to obtain her teaching certificate. I am overjoyed that she has discovered her calling. She has managed to balance work, school and play so that she is only mildly exhausted each day. Isaac is in the Fall semester of His senior year. He is so intelligent. He studies endless hours, ensuring that he understands the full content and comprehends each component and integral concept of the topic at hand. I am proud of his determination and perseverance, as I see him with the same exhausted look that my daughter wears. Maiya is in her Sophomore year at the University of Minnesota and continues to flourish there. Her artwork is beautiful and thought-provoking. She inspires me and her talent amazes me.

Although I have most recently been busy tapping on this keyboard in front of me, trying to make sense of the life I have lived, I still make lots of time for those pearls of life each day. On the weekends, when our house is full, I enjoy Saturday morning breakfast each week, courtesy of my husband's cooking skills. My momma usually comes over for our special weekly breakfast. Pancakes with fresh apples in the batter, and bacon and eggs, any way you like them. Depending on the weather and my energy level, Tim and I have some precious alone time together. Two kids hanging out. Monday through Friday, I'm pretty much on my own, except for Gio, my fearless companion. We spend time outside periodically, as Gio likes finding a nice resting place in the sun.

Neighbors often visit and we chat over the most current event happening in our lives. When I talk with people now, I forget I am wearing bandages. I have become so accustomed to having them spread across my face. It is nice to have those tiny slices of time to soak up mother nature. Time to absorb my thoughts, which don't haunt me like they used to. The ghosts of yesterday still visit me nightly and I struggle with insomnia. That is why I am always ready to arise from my slumber the moment my eyelids regress and my eyes are open to the world around me that does not hold the demons within it that my nightmares do.

Each new morning, I am authentically glad to be awake. I visit with the Lord, who has been up, waiting for me to call on Him. The more I search for God's character and explore Jesus' life on this earth, I find my desire to be obedient increases. But this life is not an audition for the afterlife. Jesus paid it all. I keep walking down the path as life rolls it out in front of me. With each fork in the road, I look for Jesus and follow Him as He leads me through this journey. During a heavy, incomprehensible storm of life, I reach out my hand to be instantly met with his strong grasp as He pulls me to safety. He has never left me, even when I thought I deserved to be one of the lost, broken souls. In this present life of mine, I do not fear. What do I have to be afraid of? I have thrust myself through the gates of hell and even there, my Lord found me. I cannot be hidden from His sight. He is my God and He strengthens me daily and is always there to be called upon whenever I am in need of his mercy and grace. He upholds me with His righteous right hand. I have been brought out of the mire, the mud and the muck and He has placed me on the Rock, which is higher than I. There, I found refuge from the storm. It stands as a tall tower against my foe.

## FACING IT

If my past resembles your present in any way, I hope that reading my story has helped you through your journey. The Lord has been sitting beside you as you have read each word. He is saying to you now, "My yoke is easy and my burden is light. Follow me."

# About the Author

A girl who has been reshaped by the Potter into a glorious work of art that radiates brilliance to all who see her beauty.

Made in the USA
Las Vegas, NV
09 August 2024

93573455R00138